COVERED...

THE FATHERLESS ATHLETE

Written by: Nigel Ali

Memoirs by: Keion Carpenter

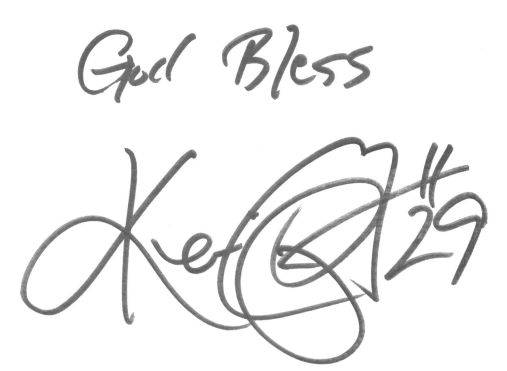

GH99 PUBLISHING
Paperback Edition 12/8/2014
ISBN: 9780692348857

INTRO

Keion Eric Carpenter was born on October 31, 1977 in Baltimore, Maryland. Baltimore City, also known as "Bmore," is a very rough place, but beneath the cluttered alleyways, liquor stores, boarded up properties and drugs, it is a beautiful city filled with children who if given the chance will rise above and succeed. The streets of Baltimore City have taken thousands of lives due to lack of leadership in the household. Fatherless children roam the streets and continue to fill the jail cells, and Keion was just like them – one decision away from ruining his life. Now, it is his responsibility and yours to save as many as we can. Being raised in a single family home is difficult and the purpose of this book is to help heal the wounds that surround many of our fatherless children's hearts. This is Keion Carpenter's story.

For those who are just seeing his name for the first time, I would like to share a little history. Just like your child, Keion was enrolled into sports at the age of three. In 1991, he played football for Woodlawn High School and with his athletic ability he received a full ride scholarship to Virginia Tech. Keion graduated from Virginia Tech with a degree in Residential Property Management. In 1999, he was signed as an undrafted free agent to the Buffalo Bills. After playing three years with the Buffalo Bills, he then signed with the Atlanta Falcons as an unrestricted Free Agent and his career ended in 2006 after multiple injuries.

<u>Words From Keion</u>

Playing football has been an absolute blessing that has allowed me to take my experiences to teach not only the game of football, but the fragile game of life through my Youth Sports and after school program, ShutDown Academy. I've been playing football for as long as I can remember and I never thought life after football could be so fulfilling. You may ask, why after all these years I am telling my story and the answer is simple. I am just like most of the sons who come to ShutDown Academy and other football institutions all over the world. Most of us grew up without fathers, and I want to use this platform to get to the bottom of it. I am not the perfect parent and the purpose of this book is not to lecture you, but to take you through the mind of your child and help you prepare.

From the moment I started playing sports, people saw something in me and I was tagged as the star athlete. I received praise from family and coaches, but I was missing the love from my father. What is the connection between successful athletes and absent fathers? Why do we all share this problem? I'm hoping this book will connect the dots. It is now 2015, and I am seeing a new breed of fatherless athletes trying to survive in a world that is moving at a pace unprecedented – and I wonder if they will make it to the professional level or succumb to the streets.

When I was first introduced to sports, I thought that I would play until I entered the Hall of Fame, but God had bigger plans for me. I want to raise the bar and encourage parents to not only use sports as a means to keep their child busy, but as a way to connect on a much higher level. To do this effectively, I must first take you back to where I started. I hope you will read this book with an open mind and use this as a blueprint on how to prevent the hidden pain your child may mask through sports.

I believe I have left enough words to express my passion for healing our athletes, but I would like to leave you with a few statistics. I hope the numbers I am presenting have declined, but more than likely, they have risen. According to the US Department of Health, 63% of those who are raised in fatherless households commit suicide. Runaway children are a product of being raised in fatherless homes and 85% of all children who are considered troubled kids by their schools are raised in fatherless homes. Lastly, 80% of rapists emerge from fatherless homes.

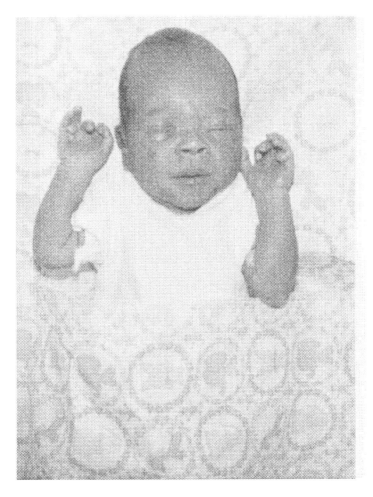

"Every child is born innocent and full of promise."

−K. Carpenter

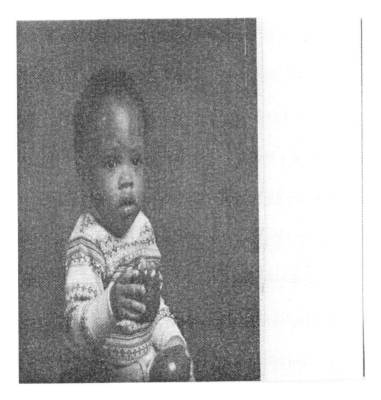

"How could anyone turn their back on something so innocent?"

−K. Carpenter

"A father should be on the receiving end of every child's steps."

−K. Carpenter

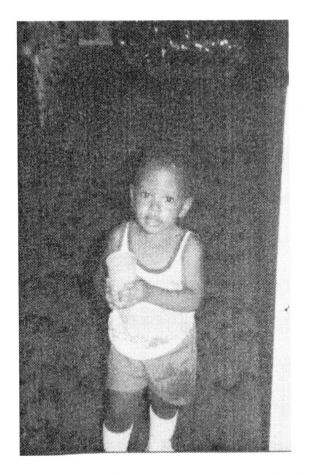

"From the moment I left my mother's womb, God had a plan for me."

−K. Carpenter

CHAPTER ONE

I vividly remember being introduced to sports in 1980. I was three years old, and I knew nothing about sports besides watching my uncle's yell at the big screen television in my grandparent's living room. When I was young, my uncles would toss me around like a ragdoll. My mother hated it, but she did not understand that is what boys did and how we behaved. I loved being around my uncles because when I looked up, I saw men who looked like me. Once they introduced me to basketball, I fell in love with the game instantly.

I remember playing basketball in the yard with my uncles and wishing I was tall enough to compete. When they dribbled the ball, I chased them around reaching for their ankles and tugging on their shirts.

> "At this age, it did not really dawn on me that I had an absentee father."
>
> -K. Carpenter

My mother told me when I was young I was extremely competitive. Maybe she was right since I still remember the joy I felt the first time I took the ball from one of my uncles. I'm sure he allowed me to take it, but it did wonders for my confidence. I would spend hours outside dribbling and trying to shoot at a rim that appeared to be in the heavens, but I did not care. In my mind, I was six−foot−four and I envisioned myself hanging on the rim like my favorite basketball heroes.

Having an athletic child was not easy for my mother, so when I turned five years old, she enrolled me into a recreational basketball league. It gave me something to do and it gave her a few hours of peace. Well, sort of. Now that I have children who play sports, I understand the toll it takes on a parent. As if a full workweek is not enough, taking your child to practice for two hours doesn't leave much time for you to relax. But, if you love your child, that is what you have to do.

"Working with children is worth every minute and a 13−0 Season is the payoff."

−K. Carpenter

Parents stand outside in the rain, snow, and blistering heat just to allow their children to feel free and burn off the fire they possess from within. To this day, I cannot understand how a father could choose to not be present in their child's life. As a man, what better way to bond with your child than in sports? Every child isn't athletic and destined to make it to the highest level, but if your child shows the slightest interest in any sport, you should support it one hundred percent.

Even though my mother worked multiple jobs to support me, she made sure she was present at every practice and game just like you do for your children, and I am living proof that the rewards are worth it. One of the most amazing things in the world is watching a bunch of toddlers trying to play sports. For forty-five minutes, we watch our innocent children run up and down. Naturally some are better than others. The score of the game does not matter; what matters is exposing our children to wins and losses and teaching them how to work as a team.

Since I played basketball with my uncles and practiced dribbling in my grandmother's driveway, I had a slight edge over the rest of the children. I dribbled around my opponents and after stealing the ball from my uncles, taking the ball from a five–year–old was a breeze. One day after practice, I remember hearing my coaches telling my mother I was "special" but I didn't really know what that meant. To me, I was just playing basketball, but to everyone else – I was a rare talent. While most children were in bed, I would stay up all night with my uncles and watch my favorite basketball players on television analyzing their every move. The following day, I would run outside and try my best to emulate what I saw on television. The more I practiced, the closer my basketball shots were getting to the rim. I wanted my uncles to cheer for me like they cheered for their favorite player. I wanted to make them proud, so I became obsessed with sports; I wanted to be the best. At this age, I came to the conclusion that no one likes a loser.

One evening, while my uncles – Linny and Buzzy – were watching a game, I ran upstairs to my room and drew a stickman picture of myself. When I was finished, I gave my uncle, my grandparents, and my mother their very own personalized stickmen. My uncles were so occupied with the Celtics versus Lakers game that they took my drawing, smiled, and laid it down on the table. I was slightly disappointed but I knew better than to interrupt my uncles during a big game. My mother could see I was very proud and that I was expecting more, so she put her hands on my face.

"What's this, Keion?"

"It's my basketball card," I replied.

My mother gave me the biggest hug she could muster and kissed me on the cheek. "I want my card autographed."

For a brief second, I was a star athlete. I zoomed back up the steps and returned with a black marker. I carefully signed my name, handed my mother her basketball card and she jumped up down like she won the lottery. She gave my little ego exactly what it needed. The seasons were beginning to change and football season was on the horizon, but that wasn't the only thing that changed in my grandmother's home. It was time for my uncles to leave the nest; college or the military were the only ways to accomplish this mission. This affected me greatly, as I was losing the men in my life. As they pursued their dreams, I often found myself sitting on the couch alone thinking about my father. Who is going to play basketball with me? Who was going to toss me in the air and give me the tough love that I desperately needed? The first person to see this void was my grandfather Lindbergh Carpenter Sr., may he rest in paradise.

My grandparents meant the world to me, and my grandfather was the perfect example of what it meant to be a man. He was the backbone and represented that with every breath he took. He wasn't a selfish man and every chance he was given, he tried to instill those values into my head. My grandfather was a calm man. He spoke with love, but he was stern. He couldn't toss me in the air like my uncles or motivate me like my coaches, but he was filled with information and he taught me how to become a thinking man. He taught me the principles of life outside of sports. He taught me about pride, integrity, and making my word as good as my heart. My grandfather knew I was talented, but he didn't see an athlete. He saw a misguided soul and he took it upon himself to mold it the best way he could.

My grandparent's instilled rich family values and they believed in the power of eating together. Every Saturday morning, my grandfather woke everyone up to the smell of his famous pancakes. My grandmother, Christine Carpenter, would add the finishing touches with her perfectly seasoned cheese eggs, sausage, and bacon. Needless to the say, the Carpenters knew how to chow down. Unfortunately, the hole I had for my father didn't allow me to accept the love I received on a daily basis. One morning after breakfast, I walked into my mother's room and sat down next to her while she folded clothes.

"My father don't love me?"

I could see my mother trying to formulate the right response. She didn't want to lie, but she didn't want to tell the truth because she didn't know. She placed her arm around my shoulder and pulled me close to her and said, "Some men are not ready to be fathers, but it doesn't mean that he doesn't love you. Okay?"

17

"Is he ever going to come to one of my games?"

"I don't know, Keion, but don't let that discourage you. You are still a wonderful child."

"But if I'm so wonderful, why isn't he around? At least some of my teammates have seen their fathers."

"No one can force your father to do the right thing. He has to make that decision on his own, but don't you wait. You have to live your life and one day you're going to be a father and you make sure you don't make the same mistakes."

> ### Coaches Corner
>
> Your job as the single mother is not to replace what the father can provide, but prevent the pain from lasting another day.

I could have asked my mother questions all night and I'm sure she would have answered each one. The conversation I was too afraid to have with my mother wasn't as bad as I thought. Did it completely heal my wound? No, but it was such a relief. That conversation was thirty years ago and I remember it like was a yesterday. Single mothers shouldn't be afraid to have this important conversation with their child. There is no magic word or phrase that will fix everything, but a simple conversation along with reassurance will last him forever. Understand that once you have "the conversation" with your child, you cannot go back to your normal routine. You have opened the gates to a topic that your child was too afraid to speak about.

Your child is going to bombard you with questions, so answer them all. And when your child is finished, have some questions of your own. My mother wasn't fond of letting me drift too far from the house, but after our conversation, her trust for me grew and she knew it was time to loosen up her leash. Now, instead of dribbling in my grandmother's yard, I was dribbling to the basketball court in my neighborhood where I played with my friends until I heard her scream my name. I lived and breathed basketball the entire summer until old man winter showed his face, but I didn't care about the freezing wind. I was so obsessed with getting better I would play in the snow. Eventually, my mother put an end to that and I felt like someone had died. The basketball season was officially over, and I had nothing but time on my hands.

After dragging my feet around the house for what seemed like an eternity, my mother walked into my room. She knew I was upset that I couldn't go outside and practice, but she was too busy at work to deal with my boredom. In my mind, every day I wasn't outside dribbling or attempting to make a shot, I was losing my skills. This caused me to become frustrated. On this particular cold winter night, I tossed my miniature basketball up against the wall. My mother sat at the edge of my bed holding a football in her hands.

"It's football season," she said.

I continued to toss my basketball up against the wall. "And?"

"I know you like basketball, but the season is over. You can't just sit around this house with an attitude."

"Can I go outside and dribble for a little bit?"

Whenever my mother got upset, she had this way of cutting her eyes in my direction. I knew I was two seconds from being slapped. In her work uniform, she stood and snatched my basketball out of midair.

"No, it's too cold. Do you wanna freeze to death? Who's gonna take care of you if you get sick?"

"You," I mumbled under my breath, but the thought that ran through my mind was, *Where's my father?* However I was too afraid to say it.

"I know you're missing your uncles, Keion, but you have to adjust to how things are now."

My mother wasn't really asking me to play football; she was telling me. I liked football, but I was good at playing basketball. I wondered if my father was an athletic person. Maybe football was the game that he played. I had this sudden interest in the game. I grabbed the football, stared at it and envisioned how it would sound and feel if he presented playing the game of football instead of my mother. Would I have agreed instantly? More than likely, yes. These moments are why a father is so important to an athlete. An active father would have discussed with me why change is good and he would have given me the courage and confidence to try. My mother tried her best, but I needed my Alpha Male to be the voice of reason.

Weeks later, my mother took me to the Woodlawn Recreational Football Field. I immediately noticed that fathers were absent. Ironically, I felt a sense of relief because I wasn't alone, but I was still confused as to why. The football field was filled with mothers trying to attach their little boys to anything with testosterone. I was no different. Whenever I watched football on television, men were everywhere. The only women who were present on the field were cheerleaders. All those years, I had

20

gone throughout life with this understanding that my mother was all I needed but I was clearly wrong. Those feelings I felt when I was alone in my room tossing my ball against the wall were confirmed.

I did as I was told and now. I was a football player. I was still a scrawny five–year–old kid, so my helmet weighed almost as much as I did. I was nervous and even though my mother held my hand, I desperately needed a man – a father to escort me onto the field.

"Are you okay?" she asked.

I wanted to tell her "no," but I didn't want my mother to feel like her efforts weren't enough. I was suppressing my feelings for her, but I was unaware I was opening the hole in my heart. She squeezed my hand tightly although I resisted, she pulled me to what would become my future. Watching football on television looked like fun, but being on an actual field was a completely different experience. I watched the older kids slam into each other and I immediately became afraid. Even though my uncles tossed me in the air, it didn't prepare me for being tackled.

With my stomach in knots, I looked up at my mother and mumbled, "I don't wanna play."

After she paid the registration fees and took off early from her second job, that was the last thing she wanted to hear. She would consider the next words out of her mouth a pep talk, but to me, they sounded dangerously like a threat. Long story short, I was going to play whether I liked it or not. She squeezed my hand and it felt like my bones were breaking. She then walked me further onto the field until we stood in front of Coach Marvin Brown.

"Hey, little guy! Are you ready to play football?"

I looked up and all I saw was an energetic guy with a whistle, but later in my life he would play a very important role as my first father figure. Coach Brown tried his best to fill that void with all of the fatherless children on my team, but he was most needed in our homes. Every day after a game, win or lose, he gave us words of encouragement. Back then, I didn't understand why Coach Brown was so animated, but now I realize his purpose was to build up our confidence regardless of our individual circumstances. With my uncles gone, and my grandfather only being able to do so much Coach Brown was exactly what I needed. I held onto his every word. At practice when I heard him scream, "Good job, Keion," it kept my mind from wondering about my father.

Now that I am responsible for my own youth organization, ShutDown Academy, when I meet a children who do not have a father, I immediately attach myself to them because I understand what goes through their minds. They may be children on the outside, but inside of each of these children are some questions only a man can answer. Coach Brown wasn't a healer and neither am I, but just like Coach Brown, I try my best to remind the children who do not have active fathers that life will and must go on. Too often, I can see the pain on their faces and I ask myself the same questions that haunted me for most of my life. Where are their fathers? What could possibly be more important than a piece of you? I often hear people say if a child has an active father in their life then that child is lucky. Having a father should not be a form of luck; it should be the norm.

I remember my first tackle during a game and watching Coach Brown jump up and down like we won the championship. I remember seeing the joy on my mother's face. After a game win or lose, she would lift me off my feet and twirl me in the air. I didn't fall in love with sports because I loved the game; I fell in love with sports because it made the

22

people around me proud. As I slowly made my progression to the game of football, my bedroom wall began to fill up with my favorite players.

CHAPTER TWO

"My mother's love never took a break."

−K. Carpenter

At home, I was a pretty decent kid, but the pain I felt was beginning to show. I became a handful, and at times too much for my mother. My uncles tried, Coach Brown was there, but where was my father? When will he pick me up and embrace me after a game? When will he buy me some candy from the concession stand and tell me how proud he is of me? Obsessing over these questions filled me with sadness, but I did not know why. I didn't need for anything; I ate, my mother made sure I had decent clothes on my back, and I was loved. So what was that feeling of emptiness I felt in the pit of my stomach, and why did it keep haunting me? Parents, imagine your child laying in bed with this on his mind. He is fighting this secret war and some of you have no idea.

I remember waking up in cold sweats after having dreams of seeing my father waiting for me in the end zone. He was a tall muscular image with his hands out. I didn't know what he looked like, so his face was never clear and he never uttered a word but the overwhelming love I felt from his presence was indescribable. In this dream, there was no one else on the field but the stands were filled with screaming fans. My mother was there and she had this look of concern on her face. I was breathing hard and trying to run as fast as I could to get to my father but I was moving in slow motion, as if I was stuck in a pool of molasses. The scoreboard sat high in the sky, and showed zeroes. The closer I got to my father, the slower I ran. Just before I crossed the fifty yard line, I woke up to nothing but darkness.

There is a difference between being a provider and being a nurturer. A provider's strength is buying power. A nurturer's strength is love and compassion. Some parents believe that providing a roof over their child's head and putting food on the table will mask the need for a father. They're fighting a losing battle. Just because your child may still ask for their father, who has given up his responsibilities, it doesn't mean that your child doesn't appreciate you. Too often, single mothers take out this frustration on their child. To those mothers who are both providers and nurturers, you may to have to face this reality. If your son yearns to meet his dad, that hole will remain open until he does.

Parents, don't be afraid or have too much pride to address these issues with your child even if your child never mentions it. Too many children are in this position and they forced to decipher "grown people" problems. It is no secret that lack of communication has plagued the black community for eons and it all starts at home. I'm sure my mother wanted to have "the conversation" with me, but I think she struggled with exposing me to the harsh realities of an adult relationship. I was a toddler, so to her the hardest part of my day was waking up. How does a single mother breakdown a failed relationship to her child? When is the right time? I wish I could tell you, but if you choose to stay silent, it will allow the father of your child to keep hiding from his responsibilities.

Even though you are the one who carried your child for nine months and spent hours in labor, you do not need to accept all the responsibilities simply because you are receiving a financial contribution. I'm urging single mothers to open up the dialouge and get into your child's mind. Your child may smile, laugh, and thank you for everything you have done, but he will still be incomplete without the love from his father.

When football season ended, I traded in my helmet and pads for a basketball. Even though I couldn't wait to hold the basketball in my hand again and hear the sounds of sneakers squeaking against the wood floor, I was going to miss Coach Brown's presence and words of encouragement. It wasn't Coach Brown's fault that when football season ended, so did our father/son relationship. I know Coach Brown loved me but I was reminded that he was not my biological father. He was just my coach. I learned a lot from Coach Brown, and then I was no longer seeing him every day, my insecurities of not having a father figure haunted me.

Coaches Corner

Too often, mothers will fight to the end of the world for the father of their child to contribute financially, but willingly accept raising their child by themselves.

A few weeks after football season ended, I resumed having the same dreams of my father and waking in cold sweats. My emotions were like a rollercoaster ride and sports were the only thing that kept me balanced. My behavioral patterns were obvious. Whenever I had to wait for the next sport to begin, my grades suffered. I closed myself away and internalized my pain. I marked my calendar and each day that passed, I was getting closer to basketball registration. That day finally arrived. I jumped out of bed and I ran to my mother's room like it was Christmas day and banged on her door.

"Whatchu want, boy? It's eight o'clock in the morning!" she yelled through the door.

"It's Saturday, Mommy!"

"And?"

"Today is registration!"

I could hear her grumbling to herself but she was always a woman of her word. Twenty minutes later, she opened her bedroom door and she was not happy. I hated to be a burden to my mother, but I wasn't missing basketball registration for nobody.

When my mother and I pulled up to the gymnasium, I quickly opened the doubled doors and walked inside. I was afraid that playing football would have deteriorated my skills, but as soon as I smelled the gym; it felt like I never left. As I held the basketball beneath my armpit, I noticed how the bleachers were filled with mothers. Some read books, while others chatted amongst each other, and occasionally screamed out their son's name or cheered. A few of the single mothers were attentive, but most were clearly using basketball to keep their child busy.

There is absolutely nothing wrong with using sports to keep your child busy, but I would like single mothers to understand that they are competing with active fathers. For example, if Chris' mother, Sandy, is in the bleachers reading a book instead of watching Chris play, when Chris observes an active father showing interest in his son's game, this may cause insecurity. If Sandy is paying attention to her son's game, this will help Chris better deal with not having an active father. Will Chris still yearn for his father's acceptance? Of course he will, but attempting to fill the void will decrease the chances of Chris feeling unwanted. Being at the game is not the same as being engaged in the game.

> "When a child feels unwanted, they will begin to associate themselves with things that are unwanted."
>
> -K. Carpenter

As I watched my mother find a seat on the bleachers, that question was once again pounding in my head. Where is everyone's father? Are they working? Are they busy? Or, do they just not care? The seed of loneliness blossomed faster than my mind could decipher.

My awareness of what I did not have was becoming sharper, so naturally I began to seek answers. After weeks of watching single mothers fill the bleachers, I asked one of my teammates why their father never came to practice or the games. He looked at me with this blank stare and shrugged his shoulders. My conversations with my teammates continued and I learned that most of their fathers were just like mine, but they were still able to share stories about their father. That was the moment when my heart broke into peices.

Let's do a little math: there are twenty-four hours in a day and three hundred and sixty-five days in a year. That's eight thousand, seven hundred sixty hours in a year and my father couldn't give me five minutes? In this gymnasium, I came to the realization that my father and I never stood face-to-face and I took all of the blame.

The troubles of two adults fell onto my shoulders like a ton of bricks. The innocent questions I asked myself turned into nightmares and then with brutal conviction I heard voices say. *"I don't want you, Keion, and you're the reason."* My subconscious was under attack. Everywhere I went, I was reminded tmy father made a conscious decision to abandon me. Before that feeling could get any worse, Coach Buddy Norris stepped in. Coach Norris took on the same role as Coach Marvin Brown, which was to instill confidence and fill the emptiness of not having a father. Whenever I scored a basket, Coach Norris was there to encourage me the way I wish my father had and it was the greatest feeling in the world. Unfortunately, I learned to teach myself that this feeling was temporary.

Each time I scored, I felt like I was proving my father wrong for abandoning me. My war from within was getting stronger. I urge the fathers who are reading this to never let your child go through this. Age five is a very important time especially for an athletic child so if you think you're going to just pop back into their lives and everything is going to be okay, you are sadly mistaken. My grandfather once told me pain does not have an age and if it continues to go unresolved it will live with someone even in death. Do not allow your child to live with this pain when your love is the remedy. Everyone has the ability to express love. Remove your foolish pride and show your son you possess this power. For an athletic child, your love and support can be the difference between your child becoming the best player or the worst player on the team. God's purpose for your son's life will prevail whether you chose to do this or not. However, your love can help your son navigate through this intricate maze.

CHAPTER THREE

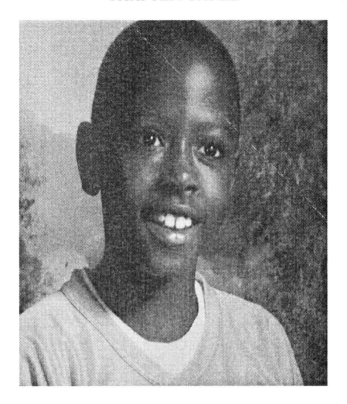

"I am no different than your child. Unfortunately, all fatherless children and athletes will not get the opportuntiy to tell their story. Most of the time, their lives are cut short or their story is told from behind bars."

−K. Carpenter

The year 1984 my life changed. I was seven-years-old and my mother stormed into my bedroom and yelled at the top of her lungs for me to get up. I hated getting up in the morning unless it was for football or basketball practice. I could sense something was wrong with her and when I asked she just shot me a look that said, "Stay in a child's place." So, I did. I placed my feet onto the hardwood floors and prepared for what today would bring. As I got dressed, I could hear my mother stomping around in her room. I didn't want to do anything to upset her, so I made sure I was on my best behavior. I kept my head down and my mouth shut.

I walked downstairs and my mother was on her knees praying in the living room. My mother has always been a God-fearing woman, but even at the age of seven, I could sense that whatever she was praying for, she really needed. After watching this strange morning develop, I finally built up enough strength to ask if she was okay. She stood, turned around and her eyes were puffy from crying. I could hear my stomach growling, but now was not the time to ask her for anything – so I simply sucked it up. My mother gave birth to me at age nineteen. She was young, frustrated and alone so it was very hard to see her hurt. Being quiet was all I could offer. She deserved a hug. I wished I were tall enough to wrap my arms around her and give her the comfort that she desperately needed.

She kneeled down and placed her warm, loving hands around my face. Her next words touched me in ways that my seven-year-old mind could not understand. She said, "No matter what happens today, don't you ever feel like you are not loved. You will always have me." I was puzzled and scared. *Am I being dropped off at orphanage?* I thought to myself. She stared into my eyes and I shook my head to her every word. Since I blamed my father for everything, I had convinced myself that he was the source of all sadness. When my mother was frustrated, I told myself that he was responsible – which only led to more emotional confusion. I was forced to put together this broken puzzle that was created because my father chose not to be there and it simply was not fair.

The ride to this unknown destination was silent. I could hear the road under the tires and the loose change moving around inside of the armrest. I wanted badly to ask her where we were going but I just stared out of the window. My stomach growled, but I would starve to keep my mother happy. A half hour later, she parked in front of a huge building that looked like a castle. My reading wasn't great, but I saw the words Circuit Court and I knew this wasn't good. I could not take the anticipation anymore. I was hungry, scared, and confused. I wasn't sure if my next words were going to get me slapped, but I didn't care.

I needed to know why we were standing in front of this very scary building. "Are you going to jail, mommy?" I asked bracing myself to feel the wrath of God, but nothing happened. *I'm still alive?* I looked over at my mother and gave her the best set of puppy eyes I could muster and blurted out, "Am I going to an orphanage?"

"Of course not! Why would you ask that, Keion? I would never do that to you. I love you with all my heart!"

"So, why are we here?"

My mother took a deep breath and exhaled. It seemed that she'd been waiting to have "the conversation" with me and that time had finally arrived. My mother came to the realization that enrolling me into sports was no longer enough. Instead of answering my question, she got out of the car and I followed. She gently held my hand, we walked up the stone courthouse steps and I was in awe at how big the buildings were. To my knowledge, this was my first trip to downtown Baltimore and it was clearly not the place for a child. My experience in downtown Baltimore taught me that the world was bigger than basketball courts and football fields. There were people everywhere, and each of their faces were filled with grief. I looked to my left and I saw a man being escorted into the building wearing handcuffs and that was all I needed to understand that jail wasn't for me.

As I watched this man being escorted by the police, I wondered if this was where my father was and ironically I became relieved. I came to the conclusion that my father was in prison and that's why he never came to see me. I convinced myself that I was here to see my father. I looked for any reason other than he simply did not want to see me. Since the age of three, I wondered where he was and now the time has finally come for us to meet. I couldn't wait to tell him I was a two−sport athlete and share the details of every game. All the love and support that my mother gave me couldn't compare to the thought of seeing my father.

The closer we got to the oversized doors of the courthouse, the tighter my mother squeezed my hand. It hurt, but I just endured the pain. She forced a smile, but I knew she was angry. She looked at me and said, "This will be over very soon and afterwards, we'll get something to eat." After a slight pause she said, "I'm very proud of you, Keion."

Moments later, a short, husky gentleman walked over to me and I looked at him slightly confused. I envisioned my dad to be tall and have an athletic build similar to a super hero, but this guy appeared to have never stepped inside of a gym.

"You need to go with him, Keion, but I'll be right back," my mother said.

I looked this man into his eyes and asked, "Are you my father?"

The husky man placed his hands on my head. "No, I'm not your father. Your mother doesn't want you to go inside of the courtroom."

The husky man continued to talk, but I couldn't hear him. I watched my mother walk inside of the courtroom and I was forced to play nice with this husky stranger. He escorted me into a room filled with kids. They served the kids snacks and allowed us to watch all the cartoons we wanted. Out of the corner of my eye, I saw a yellow and black Nerf football on top of a plastic container filled the toys. While some of the little boys played with GI Joe men and cars, I sat Indian style on the carpet and tossed the football in the air. The football allowed me to mentally escape this uncomfortable place and each time I caught the ball, I envisioned myself scoring the winning touchdown and being carried off the field by my teammates like Walter Payton.

After the paternity test and verdict, which proved Eric Carroll was my father, there I was, a small child in a room filled with kids from broken homes tossing my football in the air. My mother walked into the room and I immediately looked for my father. Instead of a warm embrace from him, my mother grabbed my arm and practically dragged me out. I hoped my mother's attitude would have changed for the better but I was wrong. Inside the car, I could see my mother fighting back tears. She was strong willed, sometimes too strong for her own good. She built a wall around her heart when it came to my father, so the last thing she wanted was a tear to roll down her face because of him. I had

36

never been this hungry before in my life. My stomach stopped growling and I felt this aching pain on the left side of my head. Each restaurant we passed, I wanted to remind my mother that she promised me some food when she finished. However, I'd rather deal with hunger pangs than a whooping.

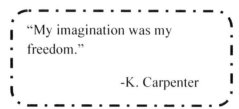

"My imagination was my freedom."

-K. Carpenter

Later that evening, I crept out of my bed and placed my ear against her bedroom door. I overheard my mother talking to one of her girlfriends on the phone. I was scared out of my mind and afraid to breath, but I was determined to get the "scoop." I knew if she caught me eavesdropping on her conversation she would turn my night into a nightmare but it was a chance I was willing to take. I covered my mouth and pressed my right ear against her door. This is what I heard.

"I had to take Keion to court with me today for his tired ass father. What am I going to do with forty dollars a month? That's not enough money to support a goldfish! What man would abandon their son? What am I supposed to tell Keion?" she asked crying.

I listened intensely as my mom described what had occurred. Since my conception, my father doubted I was his son and that day was the day I put the speculation to rest. I was ashamed it took a judge to confirm what Mother Nature already determined. When I was much older, my mother gave me the details of that day. She told me my father rocked back and forth nervously awaiting the results. It had been years since they both occupied the same space, so it was very tense. She said the only thing you could hear in the courtroom was the judge fumbling papers. The judge read the results and my father shrugged it off as if it was nothing.

I wish I never eavesdropped on my mother's conversation. The speculation was no longer and the notion that I was never going to see my father became a reality. I didn't know much about money, but knowing how much my father paid for child support made me feel worthless. My father was in the same building as me and I still didn't see him. My heart instantly turned black and shriveled up like a raisin. That day changed my life and I would never be the same again.

While my father was somewhere living his life free from responsibility at a ten dollar per week payment, my mother and I were written off like damaged goods. All of those years, my mother, my grandparents, and my coaches were filling my father's shoes and I thought I was doing just fine but having confirmation my father made a choice to abandon me was devastating. I wouldn't wish what I felt on any child. Luckily, my mother never talked badly about my father to me. She did not have to because I had heard and felt enough.

> "The worst mistake a parent can make is to assume their child is too young to understand."
>
> -K. Carpenter

Some parents speak negatively about the other parent too candidly and the effects are disastrous. Mothers, be mindful when you speak about the father of your child. To your child, your words are purer than gold and your child will hold onto every word. Learn to control your feelings about your child's father because they are watching

38

and when the father of your child decides to step up to the plate and take care of his responsibilities, you will become the blame for their relationship not working. When your son comes to his own conclusion about his father, the last thing you want is for your son to blame you for forcing your opinion of his father onto him. Your child is genetically half of their father. If your child hears you call their father "no good," then what are you saying about your child?

CHAPTER FOUR

"This picture is worth a thousand words. When I was his age, my grandfather showed me the importance of class. Too many fathers are missing this opportunity to bond with their son. This is Becoming a Man 101, and a son will always hold onto this moment."

—K. Carpenter

My grandfather, Lindbergh Carpenter Sr., had seven children of his own and I was the unofficial eighth. I've never heard my grandfather complain and no matter the situation, he never took a day off work. He was the first one up on Sunday ready to serve God. I remember standing in the doorway watching him get dressed. He was without a doubt the sharpest man in the congregation. He taught me look presentable and that dressing up for church showed respect. Whenever you walked into the house of the Lord, you should look good. He gave me this advice when I was a child and it has stuck with me to this very day. Even as adults, we are sponges, but we have learned how to prevent certain behaviors, remove negative

41

thoughts, and form our own opinions. Your child is bright, but he is not ready to take on that responsibility. Their rapidly developing minds will not stop processing what they see and hear, so be careful with what you allow your sponge to soak up.

My grandfather led the Carpenter family to church each Sunday, and it was an all−day event. We woke up at seven in the morning, arrived to church at eight o'clock sharp, and would not get home until nine that evening. If my biological father set this example, I'm sure my path and my decisions would have been much smarter. It's not just about church and sitting in the front pew for hours, but going to church also set the stage for discipline and structure. I remember waking up early just to watch my grandfather get dressed. To see the man who I admired show respect to something greater than him showed me that God was real. In my young mind, my grandfather was at the top of the totem pole, but he showed me that God is.

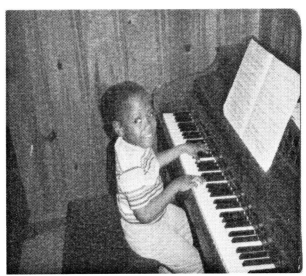

"Playing instruments helped me deal with pain."

−K. Carpenter

As a child, I knew God's name, but I did not know who God was. Since I spent so much time at church, I developed a love for instruments. I remember watching people shout in church and I was always amazed at how the music allowed people to express their love and devotion to Jesus Christ. I believed playing the drums was how I expressed my love for my Lord and Savior. To this day, I thank my grandparents for exposing me to God's grace. I later built my own relationship with God but my grandparents laid the foundation. To the fathers who are active, I do not know what your religion is, but it is vital to let your child see you worship. To your son, you are the top of the food chain and he needs to know there is someone greater. Introduce your son to God today and allow God to help you in this never ending voyage of parenting.

Fathers, there is no better way to help your child build a relationship with Christ than to see you worship. Your son is watching your every move – the way you dress, walk, talk, react, and respond are all being dissected and mentally recorded by your sons. Unfortunately, most of the fathers who are reading this book had to look outside of their own home for their father figures. It is now up to you to break that pattern. Pray with your child and let your son see you fall to your knees. Show your children you have a direct connection to the Most High. Your child will respect you until the end of time and honor you like I honored my grandfather.

CHAPTER FIVE

"At this age, I could no longer hide the pain and my questions about my father's whereabouts were beginning to increase."

—K.Carpenter

"Parents, your son will hit this stage and even though he may not know as much as you, he is ready to have "the conversation." It is vital that you do not miss that opportunity to mold his mind

before it runs wild."

−K. Carpenter

A few years after my experience at the courthouse, my mother never spoke of my father again and life went on. I still wondered about him, but since I never built a relationship with him, I told myself I wasn't missing anything. Little did I know, I was missing everything. At ten years old, I was beginning to

45

"smell" myself so I developed this attitude that you could not tell me what to do if you were not my mother. I became mouthy to my teachers and I would often lose focus on class assignments. I believe part of my anger came from knowing a child should be raised by two parents and I felt like I was at a disadvantage.

Parents, your child will hit this point and you have to be prepared. How do you prepare? You must first come to the realization that your child knows. Once you grasp your mind around that, you will know how to prevent this rebellious stage your child is almost guaranteed to face. Even when your child is not thinking about their father, they are thinking about their father. He may not have stepped up to the plate but that doesn't take away from his importance and that seems to be the battle some mothers are facing. You're doing all the work, so naturally you feel like you are taking care of all your child's needs, but sometimes, something as simple as a son sitting next to his dad is all he needs. Your role as a single mother is not to make a man become a father but to understand the importance of a father even if he is not being a man.

At age ten, sports were different and the stakes were much higher. I was very confident in my athletic abilities, but I wasn't the only one and we competed at a high level. When I was seven, my coaches didn't care if we won or lost but that was not the case for the 10−12 Cardinals. Football season was set to begin, and since my mother was busy at work, she left me in the care of Coach Hansboro. Those before him, and men like Coach Hansboro, kept me out of the streets. The streets don't care if your child has the potential to go to the next level. It will selfishly return your child in a body bag and move on to the next victim before you can arrange the funeral. The streets have killed future Hall of Famers, lawyers, doctors, and pharmacists, all because a parent chose to forfeit their responsibility. I cannot reiterate enough that it is never too late to reclaim your spot in your child's life. Do not leave this responsibility up to coaches, uncles, and grandparents.

> "Coaches are more than willing to fill in the role some parents selfishly declined, but a coach's job is to enhance what you the parent should have already enforced."
>
> -K. Carpenter

One Saturday morning after breakfast, I went outside and waited for Coach Hansboro to arrive. That day was the first day of registration and I was beyond excited. While I waited for Coach Hansboro to arrive, I held my football and pretended I was unstoppable. With my colorful imagination, I turned my grandparent's front yard into a one hundred yard football field. The bleachers were filled with screaming fans, it was the fourth quarter, my team was down by three points, and it was up to me to score the winning touchdown. I jumped over the bushes, spun off the gate, shook my way through defensive players and scored. The crowd went crazy, and I raised the ball high into the air like Deion Sanders.

In the middle of my victory dance, Coach Hansboro pulled up in his pickup truck with his sons John and Victor. I looked up to John and Victor like big brothers. I was very thankful they allowed me to share their father. Coach Hansboro exited his pickup truck and asked me to throw him the ball. Besides my uncles, Coach Hansboro was the first man to ask me to throw him the ball. I remember watching Joe Montana, and I tried my best to emulate him. I placed my fingers over the laces, cocked my arm back, closed my eyes, and let it fly. Coach Hansboro caught the ball and I could tell he was impressed. Coach Hansboro lived and breathed football and if you were good enough for him, you were good enough for anybody.

"You gotta pretty strong arm. Have you ever tried playing quarterback?"

"No," I replied. "I just wanna hit people."

"Football is about more than hitting people, Keion. You have to out think your opponent."

Coach Hansboro showed me how to properly throw the football. I didn't know which excited me more, him teaching me how to throw or having someone who showed a genuine interest.

To those fathers who may have missed pivotal years of their son's life, if you want to get your son's trust back, you have to first understand how you lost it. Come clean with your actions or lack thereof because the older your child gets, the more he is ready for an adult discussion and the reason for your absence. Another person, even your child's mom, should never be the reason you failed your child. Your son will know that this is an excuse and will categorize you as the problem.

The following Saturday, I was ready to claim my spot on the team. I woke up with this feeling to make my father regret disowning me. I was filled with so much adrenaline that I didn't stick around for my grandfather's pancakes. I got dressed, grabbed two pieces of bread, and waited by the window until I saw Coach Hansboro's pickup truck. When he arrived, I jumped in but I was not my normal jovial self.

"What's wrong?" he asked.

"I'm ready to play," I replied with my teeth gritted.

48

"Loosen up. Remember, football is serious business, but it is supposed to be fun."

At that age, I could not understand why he was expecting me to be calm. I thought football was about aggression and being better than your opponent. I didn't realize what Coach Hansboro was trying to explain until my latter years. His advice to me wasn't just about football, but life. There I was, this little wired up kid ready to release all this anger and he was teaching me how to control it. On the football field, uncontrollable anger often leads to bad plays and off the field; this same type of anger can lead to jail. My father can't give me an excuse good enough to explain why he didn't teach me these things, so I urge father's to correct this disastrous mistake.

To my every other weekend fathers, Friday through Sunday is not enough. If you are only doing what the judge has mandated, you are selling your son short and jeopardizing your relationship. Showing up to your son's game, but not making it to practice is not enough. In my opinion, a real father is a jealous one and will jump at every opportunity to help their child grow before the next man does. Which one are you, are you the jealous father or the next man? Unfortunately, most of us have become the next man and it is time for this charade to stop. When I speak of the word "jealous" I am not referring to rage but rather the passion to be the first. If your child is raised in a broken home, it is important that you instill those words of wisdom before the "next man."

Coaches Corner

Why would your child seek your wisdom if you keep allowing someone else to beat you to the punch?

While riding in Coach Hansboro's pickup truck, I didn't know what to expect. All I envisioned was me scoring touchdowns and the crowd screaming my name. We pulled up to Woodlawn Middle School and the field was filled with kids. I instantly felt butterflies in my stomach and all of my confidence vanished. Coach Hansboro unlocked the doors, but I was afraid to get out. From the passenger window, I saw kids playing catch and tackling each other without fear and I didn't feel so "special" after all. Coach Hansboro could sense I was hesitant and he had to once again step in and fill my father's shoes.

He said, "Everyone out there has a weakness and it is up to you to minimize your weaknesses and find theirs."

I took one more look at the field and I told myself if I didn't get out there and claim my spot, then my father won. I turned the man who helped bring me into this world into my archenemy. I took a deep breath, opened the car door and when my cleats touched the street all of my nervousness was gone. When we walked onto the field, Coach Hansboro introduced me as the next "big deal." The way he spoke of me made me want to prove him right. I watched the other kids playing around as if this was some sort of daycare, and for some − it was. Some of the kids were here because their mother said so, but not me. I had a purpose. I looked around at all the different coaches holding a clipboard and watching with an eagle eye at the players they wanted. I saw them writing down notes and introducing themselves to parents trying their best to recruit their child. That experience was the closest thing to a draft I could remember and even though we were just children, those coaches took it seriously and so did I.

As I walked around the field, I stared at this one kid named Andre. Andre was working on drills with his father and I was amazed at how happy they were. The joy Andre had when his father encouraged him was unexplainable. I was faster, smarter, tougher, and more skillful than Andre, but he possessed something I did not have – but mattered most; he had the love of his father on his side. To those fathers whose sons are playing football, do not allow your son to feel this way. To the naked eye, it may appear that he is running around with his friends, but he is watching how other fathers interact with their sons and he is hurt.

As I stared at Andre and his father, a great deal of sadness came over me. My spirit became broken and I wanted to go home. They say hindsight is 20/20, but I wonder if I would have had the same career had I given in to this feeling of defeat. Many talented football players have walked away from the sport simply because they didn't have their Alpha Male there to make proud. While I continued to stare at the love this man had for his son, Coach Hansboro tapped me on the shoulder and asked me if I was okay. I wanted to say, "no" but I didn't think Coach Hansboro would understand.

"Why are you staring at them?" he asked. "You're three times better than Andre."

As Coach Hansboro continued to breakdown all the flaws in Andre's technique, I wasn't listening. All I saw was a father having a good time with his son, which is the true meaning of the sport. It didn't matter that Andre was slow, clumsy and possessed no athletic ability. Andre will remember those moments with his father forever while kids like me wish on a star that is millions of miles away. I envied Andre and the few kids whose dads were present, so they were the ones I wanted to hit the hardest. I was an emotional wreck. One minute, I was telling myself that I didn't need a father and the next minute, I was hoping he sat in the bleachers cheering my name.

51

After practice, I rode in the back of Coach Hansboro's pickup truck in complete silence. Once I arrived home, my mother bombarded me with questions, but all I could think about was Andre and his father. I was obsessed with their relationship. What is wrong with me? What does Andre possess that I don't? Coach Hansboro said I was "special," but the only time I felt "special" was when I played sports, so who was I?

To the fathers with children who possess extraordinary athletic ability, it is imperative you show your child they are "special" without scoring a basket, hitting a homerun, or making the game saving tackle. As parents, we scream, hug, and toss our children into the air when they make us proud in sports, but are we showing them the same gratitude when they bring home a passing grade on a test? All I wanted to do was make my parents proud and that's all your child wants to do, so I urge you not to limit those moments of gratitude to only sports.

This confusion caused me to become quiet and my mother could sense there was something bothering me, but no one really wanted to tackle the "elephant in the room" or in my case, the "elephant" that never came into my room. I wanted to ask my mother if I was the reason my father wasn't around because if so, I wanted to do everything in my power to fix it. She would always be my mother, but things were clearly changing in our home and I needed an Alpha Male to explain these feelings I felt. I was beginning to require more privacy, so I began to shut my door and close myself off. I was also creating distance and making it harder for my mother to help. She thought I was just going through puberty, which I was, but I was also dealing with a much bigger issues. My home was no longer my place of serenity, but a place of confusion.

One day at practice, Coach Hansboro instructed everyone on my team to form a circle in the middle of the field for a tackling drill called the "Bull ring." For those of you who are not familiar, this tackling drill has been around for ages. The "Bull ring" is a great way for coaches to separate offensive and defensive players, distinguish the boys from the stars and the leaders from the followers. Coach Hansboro instructed Andre to stand in the middle of the circle. Andre looked at his father and timidly walked to the middle of the circle. Coach Hansboro then called my name and I could see the fear in Andre's eyes. The opportunity had finally arrived for me to release my jealous rage and show Andre's father that I was the "special" one.

Andre's dad stood in the distance and I heard him cheering Andre on as if he had a chance. Andre wanted to go home, but because his father was there, he had to "man up." Andre's father was very athletic, so naturally he expected his son to carry on the tradition, but this was clearly not the case. Coach Hansboro blew the whistle, and I ran towards Andre like a lion ready to destroy its prey, but I purposely missed the tackle. Andre escaped with his life and everyone was shocked. I got up from the ground and I looked over at Andre's father's face and the joy that he had was indescribable. I knew that Andre would probably never step foot onto the field during an actual game, but giving him the joy of making the best player on the team miss was something that he would remember for the rest of the season.

After practice, Andre's father pulled me aside and patted me on the shoulder. He told me not to take it easy on Andre, but that he was thankful. I thought my missed tackle was pretty convincing, but I guess even Andre's father knew his son was no match for an athlete of my stature. My coaches taught me to seek and destroy, but what kept Andre on his feet and not in an ambulance was the advice from my grandfather. My grandfather told me, "A true winner knows when to lose." That was the first and last time I let Andre or anyone else get the best of me during practice, but it was worth it and I was very proud. My message to the fathers is this, you can't fix every problem your son will encounter, but if you miss too many opportunities, he'll question if your presence is even needed.

When your child questions your presence, you'll find yourself paying your way back into their hearts and your child will take full advantage of the situation. He will accept your money and gifts with a smile, but keep you in the distance. If you aren't a credible source of information, what good are you? The first domino fell when your son realized that you didn't make him a priority and while you're counting days and weekend visits, your son is tracking your presence by the minute. The sense of urgency now is to fix your relationship with your child.

A coach only has your child's attention for a few hours a day and during that time, your sons coach and his teammates are praising him for his athletic abilities. Your son then goes home to his mother, and he is out of control. The reason for the unruly behavior is because for most of the day your son received special treatment and privileges due to his talent. Some mothers are doing an extraordinary job, but it is more impactful when a father brings their child back to earth. This is why having a father or stable father figure in the home is vital. When your child steps foot into your home, he needs to understand that his athletic abilities do not matter. As he grows taller and his mother becomes smaller, he'll need that Alpha Male to balance that understanding.

Just like your child, I earned my spot as the leader of my team. I was only a teenager, but on the football field, I was a man amongst boys and that was a difficult switch to turn off. I would walk around my mother's house with my chest poked out. Once I was tall enough to look my mother in her eyes, my attitude changed. For most mothers, this is the hardest part to deal with when raising a star athlete. A thousand beatings from a child's mother will never equal up to the sound of an active father's voice. The purpose of this book isn't to diminish the role of a mother, but to simply highlight the importance of a father.

My mother did everything she could to discipline me, but it simply didn't work. Once your son can tolerate your method of discipline, he is no longer afraid of getting caught. I was the star of my football team, the star on the basketball court, and I gained a lot of attention from the girls. Star athlete or not, your child will reach this phase and you as the parent need to understand where your child is mentally before you can prepare. Do not allow your child to become a leader without your guidance.

CHAPTER SIX

"I was no longer mommy's little boy, I was #12. Years of wondering where my father was led to this young man here. Lost and frustated, but on the verge of finding myself."

                                        —K. Carpenter

Word traveled quickly around the Woodlawn Recreational League that the Cardinals had an extraordinary offensive and defensive player named Keion, and I enjoyed every second of it. The night before my first game, I felt something I never felt before. I could barely eat and all I thought about was winning. Alone in my room, I visualized every play in my mind, but I knew it was up to me to make it a reality. I still envisioned my father walking into my bedroom and telling me that I would be ok. I was setting myself up for failure. I knew my father wasn't going to walk through my bedroom door and when it didn't happen, I simply hated him more for it.

Naturally, I didn't think my mother would understand how I felt about playing my first game and honestly, I didn't want to talk to her about it. I could have called Coach Hansboro for a few encouraging words, but that was not the voice I needed to hear. Even if we didn't talk football, I needed to know my father had my back. I was tired of wishing upon a star and I decided to grow up. For a while, not having an active father took the fun out of football; it became about business, and I was going to become my own role model. I studied the game as if my life depended on it and in a way, it did. I flipped through Coach Hansboro's playbook for hours until my mother made me go to sleep.

★★★

Saturday morning could not have come fast enough. I sprang out of bed with my eyes wide and my blood was pumping. Before I brushed my teeth or washed my face, I ran to my closet and pulled out my football uniform and stared at it. My mother had just washed it, so it was spotless and smelled like laundry detergent. I had every intention of coming home without getting a stain. I had been getting dressed to play football since the age of three, but this day was different. I was the quarterback, so every offensive snap had to go through my hands, which meant every play and all eyes were going to be on me. There was no room for mistakes.

I put on my pants and stared at my reflection from the tall mirror nailed to the back of my bedroom door. This was the first time that I saw what Coach Hansboro and my teammates saw − a football player. Before going downstairs, I fell to my knees and prayed that I threw every touchdown possible. I knew my request was pretty large, but it was worth a try. I grabbed the rest of my equipment, ran downstairs and waited for my mother to awaken. My game didn't start until eleven, but I was fully dressed and ready at eight thirty. Forty−five minutes later, my mother slowly walked downstairs scratching her eyes.

"Whatchu doing up so early?" she asked.

I was so upset that I crammed my mouthpiece into my mouth to keep from saying something that would keep me from playing. To my mother, I was just Keion, but to my teammates, I was the "head honcho." While she prepared breakfast, I paced around her tiled floors in my cleats. Instead of eating, I sat outside on the porch and daydreamed. An hour later, my mother finally opened the door. She sat down next to me and put her arm around my shoulder. She knew I was irritated, but she also knew that I would get over it. Even though I was fully dressed and ready for war, I was still just a confused, fatherless twelve−year−old boy.

She asked with a huge smile on her face, "You ready?"

I wanted to say, *Hell yeah*, but I mumbled, "Yes."

My mother then slapped me on the back trying her best to mimic my coaches. She jumped off the step and pretended like she was a wide receiver. "Throw the ball!" she yelled.

58

I couldn't help but laugh. My mother wasn't the most athletic woman in the world, so she ran around the yard in a zigzag pattern waving her hands wildly in the air. These are the moments why I loved my mother so much. She knew she could never fill my father's shoes, so instead of speaking badly about him, she did what she could even if it meant she had to run around the yard looking ridiculous. I stood, wrapped my finger around the laces, and lightly tossed her the football. Surprisingly, she caught it, ran to her imaginary end zone, spiked the ball, and did this weird chicken dance with her legs.

Normally, Coach Hansboro would drive me to the field, but my mother wanted to be present with me from beginning to end. We arrived at Woodlawn Middle School at ten fifteen in the morning and the field took on a different aura.

> "I was so consumed with playing the perfect game, that I forgot football was supposed to be fun and my mother gave me the laugh and motivation that I needed. Thank you, Mommy."
>
> -K. Carpenter

It was game time. Cheerleaders practiced their chants while food, candy, and beverages were being sold at the concession stand. This was my first taste of the football business. Each team prepared for their first matchup and the atmosphere was tense. As I looked out onto the field, there was one voice that stood out and this voice came from Coach Mark Green. I never played for Coach Green, but the way he jumped into his team's faces and grabbed their jerseys when they messed up or made a play was mesmerizing. If you played for Coach Green, you had to have heart, enjoy the pain and risk your body for the "big play." I yearned for his aggressive knock—your—head—off mentality, but at the quarterback position it was my job to avoid physical contact at all costs.

During practice, I would ask Coach Hansboro to let me play the linebacker and kick returner positions, but he just gave me a look that said, "You're too important to get hurt." Even though I understood his decision, I hated that look. I hated that look mainly because I didn't want my teammates to think I was a prima donna, and I wanted to be treated equally. Whenever we played Coach Green's team at practice, Coach Green would pump up his best players to hit me as hard as they could. I knew he was testing me, but I quickly showed Coach Green that I was a gladiator and I gained his respect.

Our game was scheduled to start in twenty minutes and I was ready to show the world what I had. Before our game, Coach Hansboro called us into a huddle. He wasn't as aggressive as Coach Green, but he always knew how to make our blood boil. As Coach Hansboro lectured us on the importance of our first game, I looked around our huddle and we were surrounded by single mothers. They camped out with lawn chairs, ready to cheer for their child. Even though I convinced myself that I was done with looking for my father, I still hoped that he would appear, tap me on the shoulder and introduce himself. If he had, I would have forgiven him for every second that he missed. That's how much I loved this person who I never met. Again, he didn't show — so I was fueled with anger.

I put on my helmet and was transported into a different world. I knew that once that whistle blew only I could help me and for some odd reason, I liked it. I found peace from inside of my helmet. I didn't need my mother or my father; I was in my absolute comfort zone.

People looked at me to make a difference and on the field, and I was the adult amongst boys. It was an amazing transformation for me and surreal to go from little Keion to the leader of my team. Before the kickoff, I walked over to Coach Hansboro and I asked if I could be on the return team. He gave me "the look", but I knew if I got my hands on the ball, I would score. Minutes before we took the field, Coach screamed out my name. I ran over, and he uttered the words that I'd been waiting for.

"I want you to return this kickoff," he said.

"Really?"

"I can't afford you getting hurt, so run towards the sideline and get out of bounds."

I said, "Okay," but running to the sideline was not an option. I was going to score. I ran out onto the field and I got in position. I looked around and I saw the parents from the opposing team screaming. Just as badly as I wanted to embarrass their child on the football field, their child wanted to put me in an ambulance. I looked to my left and I saw my mother's mouth moving. I'm sure she was screaming my name, but I couldn't hear a thing. My heart pounded and my life was caught in−between the dashes. I didn't see anything but the end zone.

The referee walked onto the middle of the field and blew his whistle. Moments later, the ball was in the air and coming my way. "C'mon, Keion," I repeated as if that was going to help me catch the ball. Right before the football fell into my hands, everything slowed down. I looked around the field to see how my blocks were developing and I saw the gap. With my helmets tunnel vision and swift agility, I was at the fifty−yard line before I could blink. I vaguely heard the cheers, and all I saw was the end zone. The closer I got, I couldn't believe no one managed to even touch me. "Am I that fast?" I immediately thought about the dreams I had about my father waiting for me and I ran harder.

When I crossed the end zone, a huge sigh of relief came over me. Ever since I was three, I envisioned myself scoring a touchdown and here I was in the end zone living out my dreams. I dropped the ball, turned around, and I fell in love with what I saw. Everyone on my sideline was cheering and jumping up and down like they won the championship. To me, all I did was score six points, but to everyone else, what I did was amazing. I looked over at the sideline and my mother's face was priceless. I vowed that if getting into the end zone would bring this much joy, I needed to get there as much as possible. My teammates bum rushed me until we all fell to the ground and then the worst possible thing happened. One of my teammates was penalized for holding.

The celebration quickly turned into a war of words and I'd never seen adults act in such a way. They screamed at the top of their lungs at the referee and the opposing team as if they wanted to fight each other. That was the moment I realized how emotional the game of football was, and I loved it. One of my teammates was penalized for "holding" so my touchdown was erased off the board and something about seeing my six points turn to a zero did not feel right. That penalty backed us up ten yards, so I was deep in my end zone. Coach Hansboro wanted to pull me out of the game, but I insisted on staying on the field. I knew the opposing team was coming to tear my head off. I looked over at my mom, but this time I saw that she was worried, as if she knew I was going to get "cracked."

Within seconds, the football was spinning in the air, but this time, I didn't have time to look around to find the gap and I knew I was in trouble. While my teammate's risked their bodies to help me gain yards, I saw a slight crease out the corner of my eye. I made one cut, and

I was off to the races. The closer I got to the end zone, the more my confidence increased. When I finally reached the end zone, I turned around and there was complete mayhem. To everyone else, I had done the impossible, but to me, I just wanted my six points back on the scoreboard. In sports, every child has this moment and to those fathers who missed their child's "moment," your presence or lack thereof may have determined their fate.

CHAPTER SEVEN

Becoming a twelve-year-old football star was an amazing feeling. I made Coach Hansboro proud and my teammates loved me. I always wanted the ball to be in my hands and I wanted all eyes to be on me, but I quickly learned that being "special" came with a flipside. My jersey became a target and whenever someone's child tackled me, I would hear the opposing team's parents and coaches screaming as if I wasn't human. "Knock him out," they yelled at the top of their lungs and pumped their fists as if they wanted to run out onto the field themselves. I was just a pre-teenager trying to make my mother proud, but to the opposing team I was a threat who needed to be stopped. Monday through Friday I was just Keion, but Saturdays belonged to #12; when my jersey took on a life of its own. Whenever I stepped onto the field, the older kids would yell out my jersey number instead of my name. This overwhelming attention gave me a certain swag that didn't always lead to a positive outcome.

My confidence was at an all-time high. Unlike some young boys who were my age playing football, I knew what I wanted to become in life and I would stop at nothing to achieve it. My success on the football field made me feel like a man and that I could do no wrong. People looked up to me and I was just twelve years old. Parents would tell their children to be like me and it became harder for my mother to discipline me. I used to be afraid of my mother's discipline and my responses were changing from, "Yes ma'am" to "What?" The notoriety I received on the football field created a monster only a father could tame.

In Baltimore, once you have proven yourself on the football field or on the basketball court, you earned a reputation and with that reputation came the "cool kids" who always brought trouble. My mother tried her best to keep up with my teenage attitude, but I thought I knew it all and we bumped heads often.

Instead of embracing Coach Hansboro and others for stepping in to take my father's place, I self-consciously built a wall and I told myself that Coach Hansboro wasn't my father – so he was not qualified to tell me what to do. That attitude was evident in practice and later made it to the field during games. If one of my teammates messed up, I yelled and threw temper tantrums and the opposing teams loved to see me frustrated. They knew if my mind wasn't in the game, my team was going to lose and we generally did.

> "In the beginning, I was a leader, but my personal frustrations with my father turned me into a selfish competitor and I didn't care if we lost, as long as I scored."
>
> -K. Carpenter

One Saturday, I scored three touchdowns, had one interception, and numerous tackles, but we still lost the game. I snatched off my helmet and threw it as far as I could and yelled at my team. Coach Hansboro ordered my team to gather around him and kneel down, but I selfishly remained standing and looked away as if he wasn't talking to me. When Coach Hansboro dismissed the team, I walked away, but he grabbed me by the jersey. I attempted to snatch away from his grip, but he clearly showed me that I might be the captain of the team, but he was a man. With a tight grip on my jersey, Coach Hansboro escorted me away from the on-looking crowd.

"What the hell are you doing, Keion? You don't talk to your teammates like that."

I tried to fight back my tears and years of frustration, but I couldn't. My heart thumped and I took deep breaths as I tried to form my words. "It's not just a game to me."

"Look at your teammates. Is this the example you want to set? They all look up to you; you should never lose your cool."

With tears rolling down my face, I replied, "What do you want from me? I scored three touchdowns."

"I want you to remember, football is supposed to be fun."

I couldn't hold it any longer so I blurted out, "I hate losing. My father don't wanna be with a loser."

Coach Hansboro stepped back and he was forced to deal with what he knew to be true about most of the players on his team. He kneeled down and placed his hard hands against my face and said, "You have greatness in you, Keion. Your father is the one that has lost. Don't hang onto this anger; it will only stop you from reaching your full potential."

Coach Hansboro walked away and even though every word he shared with me was true, that still didn't stop the pain and emptiness I felt. In my young pre–teenage mind, I hoped if I was unbelievable on the field, somehow, the word would get to my father and he would surprise me at one of my games. I continued to set myself up for failure. For the rest of the season, I scored two touchdowns per game and the opposing teams were scared to kick the ball to me. I continued to internalize my pain and take it out on whoever was on the other side of the ball. I threw my body around without fear. I remember hitting someone so hard my nose bled but I didn't care. My heart was broken, so dealing with a little physical pain was easy. Eventually I stopped looking for my father and every touchdown I scored was my way of saying, "I don't need you."

CHAPTER EIGHT

The year was 1990 and I was thirteen years old. I only had one more year left of playing for Woodlawn Recreational then I was off to High School. I was bigger, faster, and more determined than ever. When I stepped onto the field, all eyes were on me and people from all over came to see me play. I received praise from everyone. With notoriety came girls, but this one girl in particular caught my eyes. Trisha was a few years older, but the way she cheered my name from the sideline told me she was fond of me. During my games, I used to look for my mother on the sideline, but as the season progressed, Trisha was the one who I looked for. At this age, I was very curious about sex, but without guidance, I was sure to mess up.

After my last game of the season, I saw Trisha in the distance. Normally, my mother would come over to give me a kiss on the cheek, but there was no way I was going to let her embarrass me in front of Trisha. I dodged my mother's puckered up lips, gave her a hug, and quickly made my move to Trisha's direction. I didn't know what I was going to say, but I couldn't chance not saying anything at all. I had scored three touchdowns and my team won by twenty–one points, so I had a certain swagger in my step. When I stood in front of Trisha, all my confidence disappeared like a magic trick. She waited for me to speak, but my mind was scrambled and I looked foolish with each second that passed.

"Hi," I said trying to avoid eye contact.

Trisha was so pretty she didn't have to say a word. I knew that she was only giving me the time of day because of my reputation on the football field, but I didn't care. As I admired Trisha from head to toe, I could see the envy on my teammate's faces so I basked in my glory. What better way to end a three touchdown scoring, twelve tackling football game than with a conversation with the cutest girl on the field? When Trisha spoke, I was so distracted by her bubble gum colored lip-gloss that her words sounded like Charlie Brown's teacher. I had never been with a girl before, but the feeling I felt in the pit of my stomach was clearly curiosity.

Trisha placed her hand on her slim frame, "You're really good, Keion."

"Thank you. I —"

My mother's screeching voice pierced the sky as loudly as a fire alarm. I had never been more embarrassed in my life. If teleportation was invented, I would have disappeared.

I was just a few seconds away from asking for Trisha's telephone number, but the way my mother called my voice was a clear reminder that I was still a child. She called my name again and I knew if she had to call my name a third time, it would have been disastrous. Trisha smiled; I knew if I didn't seize the moment, I would have to wait until next season. Up until this point, football was all I thought about, but after my short and embarrassing moment with Trisha — losing my virginity became my number one priority. As if dealing with my ego wasn't enough, now my mother had to deal with her sons sexual curiosities.

★★★

As time went on, my nervousness with the ladies faded and I would be lying if I said I didn't take advantage of being the star athlete. I did not have to convince a girl to hang out with me like most of my friends. I never truly understood why woman were attracted to athletes. I didn't have a dime in my pocket and I didn't wear the latest clothes, but the girls threw themselves at me. At times it was overwhelming. Imagine your little boy going to school and because of his popularity, he can have any girl that he wants.

Without the proper guidance, your star athlete can turn you into a grandparent before they graduate High School. The magnetic force between women and star athletes is an entire book in itself. The pressure these types of women put on athletes does not start when your son is making millions. It begins the moment he is labeled as "special."

In my opinion, when it comes to sex a mother's advice can only travel but so far. Not to say a mother's advice will not be effective, but a father must absolutely have "the conversation." Too many great young athletes have had to give up their athletic aspirations to become a parent. At age fourteen, I was beyond puberty and the wrong night could have altered my future.

How many fatherless children have become fathers simply because they didn't have a father? Sounds confusing? How many of the fathers reading this book were never taught how to interact with girls? Unfortunately, most have never had a conversation about sex with their Alpha Male, so they found out on their own and became fathers from lack of information.

In most broken homes, teenage sons witness their parents showing dislike for one another and those are the moments that train your son how to interact with the opposite sex. Whenever I saw my grandfather embrace my grandmother, it showed me that being affectionate was also a part of being a man.

Luckily for my mother, my infatuation with Trisha and girls paused once the brisk football season ended. Spring was in the air and the ice began to melt off the basketball courts. My second love was on the horizon. Around my neighborhood, my reputation on the football field gained me a lot of respect, but what surprised people was my ability to be just as good on the basketball court. I was the only one who could play with the older kids and that was a sign of respect in my neighborhood. I played the point guard position, which is very similar to the quarterback position, and I could handle the pressure. I had a supreme confidence in myself because I lived by one rule, "I will not lose."

The older kids respected my heart and through basketball, I made a name for myself on the street. Even though I was good at both sports, there was something oddly different about basketball. The weather was hot, the girls wore less, and the sport didn't just attract basketball players; it also attracted the hustlers. I started playing basketball in my neighborhood in Campfield, which is located in Baltimore County, but my name was slowly being talked about from the mouths of respected basketball players in the city.

It was no secret that the children who grew up in Baltimore City were more aggressive. Baltimore City was known for breeding young football players who lived in rough conditions and possessed raw talent and that fact applied to basketball as well. It was also no secret that when it came to either sport, Baltimore City and Baltimore County were rivals. The kids from Baltimore City wanted to show the kids from Baltimore County they were more skilled and prove that the kids in Baltimore County were sheltered or soft.

> "I knew if I could make a name for myself in the slums of Baltimore City, then I could make it anywhere."
>
> -K. Carpenter

Once I gained respect with the older kids in Baltimore County, I knew it was just a matter of time before I would be tested and asked to play basketball with the city kids. I didn't care because whomever I was up against didn't matter to me; a rim was a rim. One afternoon, my friends and I gathered up our best players and caught the bus into the city. The differences was immediately noticeable. In Baltimore County, basketball courts were clean, surrounded by a decent neighborhood and just a few hundred yards from a school. In the city, a basketball court was part of their neighborhood. To the kids in Baltimore County, basketball was a hobby, but to the kids in Baltimore City, it was a way to escape their environment. I stared at all the people outside and I knew I was in a different world. Tons of people stood around the basketball court while hustlers served junkies and the city girls walked around in short dresses. Where were their parents? Why did they have so much freedom? I was intimidated, but I loved the challenge my friends and I were up against.

In my neighborhood, I didn't have to ask who was playing next because I never got off the court, but playing in the city was different. I was nothing but an outsider and the wrong words could place my friends and I in a body bag. I watched drug dealers walk onto the court as if they ruled the world and in this environment, they did. There were dice games, loud music and some people smoked weed as if it were legal. If my mother knew I was here, her heart would have stopped. Ironically, being in a place she wouldn't have allowed only added to the excitement. As I walked around the basketball court, I noticed that the kids my age seemed older. I watched kids my age popping wheelies on dirt–bikes for attention and back then, we called them crazy. Now they're called the "12 o'clock boys." I thought putting on a helmet and running full speed into someone was dangerous, but that was a walk in the park to these kids. Were all of these children victims of not having a father in the household, or was this just a way of life? Just being there made me appreciate the life that my mother had provided, but I was still intrigued by the danger.

After an hour of watching this new world, it was time for my team to play. Everyone knew we were not from their neighborhood, so all eyes were on us and I loved every second of it. Just like playing football, as soon as the basketball touched my hands, I felt invincible and I was. Each time I scored, the reaction from the crowd was crazy. They weren't used to seeing "County boys" playing basketball with so much heart. The city girls pointed and I could feel their eyes scanning me from head to toe. Each time I scored, the girls would signal for my attention and the guys in the neighborhood didn't like it, but that didn't stop me from playing. During the game, I received hard fouls and angry stares from people on the sideline, but nothing was more important to me than winning.

After hours of playing, I sat down on the basketball court and this guy named Slim approached me. I didn't know what to expect, but I knew he was a drug dealer. Slim was dressed like a rapper wearing a herringbone chain, dark shades, and his cornrows touched his shoulder. In the 1990's, hip hop was changing the world and the era of consciousness and gangster rap pushed its way onto the scene while drugs were pumped into the black communities like a science project. Somehow music, sports, and drug dealing brought the community together and destroyed it all at the same time. The common denominator was growing up in a single parent home. I wonder to this day, if more fathers were present in their child's lives, would there be a "hood?" How many deaths would be prevented if an active father taught his son how to avoid meaningless conflict? I know these are loaded hypothetical questions, but think about it.

From the moment a child can understand who his father is, that father becomes superman. A father loses power and respect when he is absent, so naturally; your child looks for a new superman. We often hear the black community screaming for a leader. Why are we still waiting for someone to lead our children to the promise land? Father's, you are that leader. God gave you the opportunity to become superman to your child, so don't disappoint. Since I was a child, I have been waiting for my superman to rescue me, but as a teenager, believing in some fictitious comic—book hero was ridiculous. So there I was, playing basketball inside of a deathtrap. I was infatuated with what I didn't understand and there was no one to save me.

I never had aspirations of being a drug dealer, but Slim made it look cool. Playing basketball and football only made me cool with a specific crowd, but I learned that being "cool" in the streets was very different. Slim wore a pair of Jordan 5's and I remember begging my mother for those shoes, but she couldn't afford them. His herringbone chain laid around his neck and his high—top fade was cut perfectly. He took off his shades, pulled out a knot of money, and gave me and my friends fifty dollars each. I was reluctant to take it, but that would have been a sign of disrespect.

"What's this for?" I asked.

Slim's grin revealed his gold teeth. "I placed a bet on you and your boys, and I won." He rolled up his jacket sleeve showing his gold watch. "Y'all gotta lot of heart coming down here. Where y'all from?"

I looked Slim into his eyes and said, "Woodlawn." I waited for him to criticize us or chase us off the court, but he just smiled. In the middle of our brief conversation, Slim's pager vibrated. As if the clothes, jewelry and money weren't enough, Slim pulled out his cell phone and I was in complete awe. My mother didn't even have a cell phone, but here was this young drug dealer living better than most adults.

I thought basketball was just a game, but once Slim's fifty-dollar bill touched my hand, I was exposed. Needless to say, that wasn't the last time I earned money playing street ball.

One summer afternoon, I was lying across my bed and my mother opened my bedroom door. In her hand was three hundred dollars I had received from Slim. I jumped out of bed trying to think of a fast lie, but I kept drawing a blank. I was too young to get a job and I didn't cut grass, so all I could do was be honest. I wondered how she found it in the first place. Then I remembered she always washed my clothes. That was the moment I realized it was time for me to start doing my own chores.

As I stared with a confused look on my face, my mother's eyes cut through me like a knife. She folded the money and put it into her pocket. I knew I would never see that money again. She sat down next to me and I could sense that she didn't know what to say. My mother was always conscious about letting me grow and explore, but she was still very firm and keeping secrets in my household was an absolute "no-no." Self-consciously, we both wished there was a father figure present.

I came clean to my mother. Instead of her lecturing me, she simply told me to never go down there again and left me to myself. I loved my mother and I never wanted to disappoint her, but getting caught only made me smarter. For the rest of the summer, my friends would ask me to play basketball in the neighborhood, but I was addicted to the city life. Street ball was big business in the hood and Slim had more than enough money to go around. I had hundreds of dollars hidden in my drawer and it was all from playing street ball. I knew if my mother found out that I was still going down there, I would be in a lot of trouble. In my immature mind and lack of male guidance, I thought she was just being over protective. I wasn't breaking the law; I was just getting paid to win. I loved to win and that was all Slim and I needed to have in common.

> "Up until this point, I admired athletes like Magic Johnson, Deion Sanders, Jerry Rice, and Ronnie Lott to name a few. But my new 'superhero' was standing right in front of me, a drug dealer."
>
> -K. Carpenter

In my neighborhood, if the basketball court attracted violence, mothers would have gone to the school and raised hell until the rims were removed, but not in the city. It appeared the entire neighborhood was abandoned by the parents and there was no one to speak up against the level of poverty and violence. Were they scared, had they given up, or were the parents themselves also infatuated with the danger? In the city, the cops tried to monitor the activity that took place on the basketball court. They never had enough evidence to make an arrest and to be frank, the residents didn't seem to care.

One Friday night, I told my mother I was staying overnight at one of my friend's house, but I was actually on the bus headed into the city to play basketball. Normally, I would take my friends with me, but everyone wasn't fond of playing in the city so I would go alone. In my neighborhood, we played basketball until we couldn't see the rim or until our mothers screamed our names, but that was not the case in Baltimore City. The streets did not sleep and neither did the game of basketball. When the lights came on, the basketball court took on a different vibe. In pockets of darkness, drug transactions were taking place and hookers pleasured their customers in the nearby bushes. This place was built for the strong hearted and showing weakness would definitely put you in an ambulance.

I walked onto the court and Slim greeted me with open arms. Just like my coaches, Slim paraded me around like I was his secret weapon and I loved the attention. I was protected and being affiliated with Slim meant I was "cool". That meant everything to me. Slim was a poster child for hustlers and he represented that with every breath he took. He commanded respect and the girls flocked to him like bees to honey. Before the game started, Slim walked me to his brand new gold 1990 Acura Legend coupe with silver BBS rims. I had only seen this car in the magazines and music videos. All I had was a basketball in my hand and a bus ticket. Slim had the hottest car on the street. I had all of the athletic ability in the world, but I had nothing to show for it. My coaches, teammates, and friends told me I was "special," but as I looked at the car of my dreams, to me, Slim was the one who was special. Before meeting Slim, I was a simple teenager with simple needs, but my priorities were beginning to change.

While Slim talked on his phone, I waited patiently. Slim always treated with me respect, but as I listened to his conversation I could tell Slim was more than just a flashy drug dealer. He was a gangster. I have heard many stories about drug dealers, but hanging around Slim – I learned being slightly bipolar was a requirement in the drug business. He reached into his pocket and casually gave me one hundred dollars. Normally, Slim only paid me when I won – so I was confused by the gesture. He put his knot back into his jeans and looked me directly in the eyes.

"I gotta lot riding on this game, and I need you to do whatever it takes to win."

"How much did you bet?" I asked.

Slim grinned, "Ten thousand."

My jaw dropped. My conversation with my mother flashed in my head and had I listened, I would not be in this predicament. Letting Slim down could be bad for my health and I enjoyed pressure, but knowing that I could be the deciding factor if Slim won or loss ten grand was too much for me to handle. While Slim flicked through his stack of money, I wondered what my father would do? What did I get myself into?

The basketball game started and there was nothing fun about it. I had no one to blame. I did this to myself, so I blocked out everything and all I heard was the basketball bouncing up and down on the blacktop. I could feel Slim's eyes beaming down on me with every shot I missed, so I drove to the basket as if my life depended on it. I'm sure if my team lost, I would have lived to see another day, but I didn't want to disappoint Slim. He was my "superhero."

To the fatherless fathers. Yes, you. Ask yourself, did you look up to the drug dealers in your neighborhood? Did your infatuation with the lifestyle cause you to sell drugs yourself? If so, how many times did you escape death or go to prison? In Baltimore City, this type of lifestyle is normal and if you are not around, your son will walk the same path that you chose and he may not live to tell his story. The elements of the streets will never change; just the faces. If you allow your son to pick their "superhero," more than likely, they'll pick their neighborhood drug dealer. If you admired the neighborhood drug dealer, what makes you think your son won't? An active father can prepare his son for these situations. Even when they aren't listening, they will hear your voice when it matters.

★★★

Under the basketball courts lights, my team was down by two. My heart raced at speeds unimaginable, but I was focused. Within seconds, the game was tied and it was so tense that the loud cheering turned into an awkward whisper. Whether we lost or won, just like football, I wanted the ball in my hands. There I was, this teenager from Baltimore County, playing with people almost twice my age, a ten thousand dollar bet on the line and the next few seconds determined it all. I had the urge to vomit as sweat poured down my face. I shook my defender, crossed half court and when the coast was clear, I put up the shot. The basketball arched in the air and everyone watched with anticipation. It began to curve and I knew it was going to miss. While the basketball floated for what seemed like an eternity, all I could think about was leaving there unharmed. The basketball hit the back of the rim, but one of my teammates was there to tap the ball in and we won. The crowd burst into a loud roar. Slim and his entourage rushed onto the court. The game was over and I nearly fainted from all of the pressure.

Before this game, I was just Slim's special weapon from the county, but after this game, I earned my name. People who I thought hated me congratulated me for playing a good game and having the heart to take the shot. Being popular in my neighborhood was great, but getting respect in one of the roughest neighborhoods in the city was addictive. With a huge smile on his face, Slim sat down next to me.

"You just made me ten grand! I knew we were gonna win." Slim handed me four hundred more dollars. "This petty change. You wanna make some real money?" He showed me a vial containing a white substance.

I didn't know what it was, but I knew it wasn't baby powder. I declined and prepared for Slim to look down on me and apply pressure to hustle with him, but instead he patted me on the shoulder and smiled.

"Don't be like me, Keion. You gotta future."

I wanted to stick around and enjoy the celebration, but my bus was coming. "I gotta go, Slim."

"Why? The party just begun!"

"My bus is coming."

Slim burst into laughter. "I can't let the man who just won me ten grand catch the bus. I'll take you home."

During the ride to the other side of town, I watched Slim's left hand grip the steering wheel while he blasted his radio as loudly as it could play. I could not help but wonder how Slim became a notorious drug dealer so young. When we pulled up to my home, the kids in my neighborhood stared with envy and I felt like a superstar — until I saw my mother standing in the doorway. I knew I was in trouble, so I placed the money I won inside of my shoe and got out of the car. I didn't know what to expect, so I pretended like everything was ok. When I reached the door, my mother snatched me up by the shirt and pushed me inside of the house.

"Who the hell was that, Keion? And you better not lie."

"That's just a friend of mine. He picked up me up from the bus stop."

My mother just stared. "You must think I'm stupid. I told you not to be around people like that."

"Like what? You don't even know him. I'm not a baby anymore."

Before I could finish my sentence, she slapped me so hard my vision was blurry. "Don't you lie to me, boy!" She hit me again, but I just balled up and screamed. I continued to plead my innocence, but that only made things worse. "Get upstairs before I kill you."

With a few minor whelps forming on my arm, I walked upstairs with a smirk on my face. I walked into my bedroom, and locked the door. I pulled the money out of my shoe and started to count it. As I stared at the wad of cash, my posters of my favorite players was beginning to lose value. My mother couldn't prove that I had done anything wrong, but she knew that anyone who drove a brand new Acura was not the company she wanted me to keep. Soon, I began to take pride in all the things I could accomplish without my parents. My father's child support payments increased to twenty dollars a week and here I was with five hundred dollars in my hand. In my mind, I was more of a man than my father was.

Soon, my visits into the city were no longer about playing basketball, but just being around Slim. His lifestyle was flashy, fast and he possessed the same "I will not lose" attitude I had in sports. Unfortunately, in Slim's line of "work," losing often meant death or prison. Slim was a leader and the girls didn't love him as much as they loved his money. Being around Slim affected me in ways that only a father could fix. I was introduced to teenage girls with little to no respect for themselves and I began to believe that all women should be treated like objects. Slim was just living his life, but I was picking up his bad traits. I watched how he treated girls like they were beneath him and it was mesmerizing how they accepted their role as his "side—piece." At this tender age, I was a sponge and ambition pumped through my blood non—stop. The line between right and wrong was blurred and I was falling deeper into the nothingness they called the "hood."

My basketball skills gave me a pass to hang around Slim's neighborhood. There was nothing more mesmerizing than watching someone so young with so much power. The houses in Slim's neighborhood were boarded up and junkies dragged their feet from spot to spot while prostitutes posted up on the corner with battered faces. Slim was only twenty years old and he was already a street legend. He paraded me around the neighborhood and he loved telling people the story of how I helped him win ten thousand dollars. I didn't quite understand why Slim took such a liking to me, but he was quickly becoming a father figure.

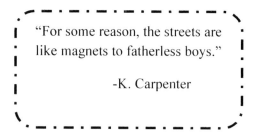

"For some reason, the streets are like magnets to fatherless boys."

-K. Carpenter

Slim introduced me to his girlfriend's and they were some of the prettiest, full—figured women I had ever seen. I would spend hours watching Slim's drug operation. People feared him and they showed him the upmost respect while handing him knots of money. Sometimes, Slim would ask me to stand on the corner and lookout for cops and I was so

81

infatuated, I would have done anything he asked. Since the age of three, I clung onto the different men in my life and Slim was no different. Slim didn't have a purpose like Coach Brown and Coach Hansboro. Slim was just Slim, a conniving drug dealer who would use anybody to make a dollar. I knew that I was disposable to Slim and ironically that fueled me to want to be closer to him. He didn't fill my head up with falsehood; he spoke and treated me like an adult, and I enjoyed his raw perspective.

One Saturday afternoon, I grabbed my bag and headed towards the front door when my mother called my name. I already had my lie ready to go, but she was two steps ahead of me. I was dressed to play basketball, but inside of my duffle bag were clothes to hang out with Slim. For weeks, Slim had been talking about this party he was having at his house and nothing was going to prevent me from going. My mother sat down on the couch and I knew this wasn't going to go well.

She looked through me like was a piece of glass. "What's gotten into you, Keion?"

"What?"

"Don't say "what" to me, boy!"

"My bus is coming in twenty minutes, mommy."

"Sit down; you think you got life figured out, huh? I know that you're still going down there. Do you wanna go to jail or get killed?"

"I'm just playing basketball, Ma."

"Oh really? I heard that you're standing on the corner in a rough neighborhood. Is that true?"

"I was just talking with a few friends, that's all."

"Friends? Is this the same friend that drives that brand new Acura?"

"Yeah." I replied with my hand over the doorknob just in case I got a chance to leave.

"You don't belong down there, Keion. It's dangerous. That boy is not your damn friend. You have plenty of friends in your own neighborhood, so why do you have to go down there?"

"Dang, I'm just playing basketball! You gotta trust me."

"You think you're a big boy? There are two ways to learn, Keion – the easy way and the hard way."

"I'm not doing anything wrong."

"That's what they all say." My mother walked into the kitchen and began to start dinner. "A hard head makes for a soft butt." She yelled, "bye."

My mother was right. I was hard−headed and the only thing that was going to save me was a "wake−up−call." I was tired of being little Keion; I was ready to be a man and that wasn't going to happen in my bedroom. I took one more look at my mother, opened the door, and left.

★★★

When a child becomes a teenager, it is harder to advise them on life lessons and sometimes you have to allow them to fail. A lot of single mothers find themselves in this position because their son is growing into a man and his curiosity is like a trick birthday candle that continues to burn. At some point, a single mother has to allow their child to blow it out. I believe a conversation like this with an active father would be slightly different. First, an active father has already established that he is not just giving advice, but laying down the law. My mother could've easily forced me to stay inside of the house, but that would have only increased my infatuation with the streets. It is a huge gamble for a single mother to allow their son to learn from their mistakes, but without an active father present, this may be the only method you have to prove that mommy is always right.

Even though I was severely missing a father in my life, I was beginning to enjoy not answering to another parent. Single mothers beware. Your son will soon hit this point in their life when their athletic ability will open doors that they are simply not mature enough to walk through. It was difficult for my mother to get through to me because coaches, girls, teammates, friends, and drug dealers treated me like an adult. My mother could talk until she was blue in the face, but as long as she didn't make me stay in the house, I considered that a victory.

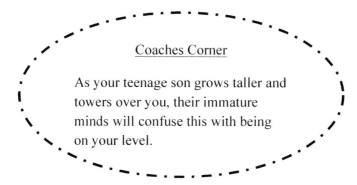

Coaches Corner

As your teenage son grows taller and towers over you, their immature minds will confuse this with being on your level.

After my brief conversation with my mother, I ran to the bus as fast as I could. While on the bus, I looked out the window and I watched the neighborhood change from homes with yards, to destroyed buildings and liquor stores on almost every corner. When the bus stopped at a red light, I looked to my left and I saw a homeless man lying on the bench. I wondered if this homeless man was the product of a fatherless home. As the bus pulled off, the homeless man looked up and I felt like he was looking directly at me. At this moment, I vowed to use my athletic abilities to keep me out of poverty and ironically this bus was taking me to the very place that I was trying to escape.

My bus arrived at North Avenue. I grabbed my bag and basketball and walked towards Slim's neighborhood. I had done this so many times that I wasn't afraid anymore, but I had many questions running through my mind. How did this neighborhood get like this and who was responsible?

Instead of walking to the basketball court, I walked to Brian's house. Everyone called him Butter. Butter was fifteen years old and he sold drugs for Slim. Butter's father was killed and his mother was on drugs. From the first day I met Butter, I could see the pain his eyes, but I never knew where this pain came from until he invited me into his home. Dribbling my basketball, I followed Butter to a home that almost looked abandoned. The windows were cracked and some were covered with plywood. I could hear rats running beneath the porch and I was mortified, but this was normal to Butter. He pushed opened his door and his mother sat nodding in and out of consciousness with a syringe needle and drug residue on the old coffee table in front of her. I immediately felt sorry for Butter, but I pretended to not be phased by this horrific sight.

"Wait right here," Butter said before running upstairs.

I stared at Butter's mother and I instantly fell in love with my mother all over again. I couldn't imagine coming home and seeing my mother unconscious from drug use. Minutes later, Butter ran downstairs and opened the door to leave without saying a word to his mother as if she was a stranger.

"Keion, you going to the basketball court?" Butter asked.

"Yeah, I'm going to see what's up with Slim first. Then I'll be over."

I walked towards Slim's neighborhood and there he was posted up on the corner watching his drug enterprise. As I got closer to Slim, I noticed that there was something different about him. He constantly looked around as if someone was watching him. I had never seen him nervous. While Slim watched his block and collected money from his workers, I dribbled my ball. It was eighty-five degrees outside and he stood with his right hand inside of his jacket. He was overdressed for one purpose, to conceal his weapon.

"I don't want you round here anymore," Slim said looking left to right. "I'm serious, Keion. I like you, but this ain't the place for you."

I stopped dribbling the basketball. *Why was he saying this to me? What did I do?* My feelings were hurt, and I was confused. I was afraid to ask why because no one questioned Slim's authority. He was my role model, so how was I going to be become a man if I couldn't watch his every move? What about the people who I called friends and my popularity on the basketball court? Why would Slim take this away from me? The disappointment I felt was very similar to the pain of abandonment I felt from my father, and it seemed like everyone I clung to had an expiration date. Even though I made Slim thousands of dollars playing basketball, I was no longer good enough. For the rest of the evening, Slim's demeanor was cold and his words were few. I continued to watch him sell drugs and I thought of every way possible to keep the friendship I thought we had. He walked over to me with a huge knot of money in his hand.

"Can I help you?" I asked.

Slim looked at me with a weird smirk on his face. "Help me do what?"

"I wanna stay out here with you and make some money."

"This ain't the basketball court, Keion. You're in a warzone. You have a future that is bigger than standing on the corner with me."

"Just tell me what to do and I'll do it."

"I appreciate that, but this a crazy world and sometimes you gotta do the wrong thing to get the right results." Slim pulled out a one hundred dollar bill. "Are you willing to kill for this piece of paper?"

"No."

Slim pointed to a guy leaning up against the wall. "That junky will kill you for this one hundred dollar bill and he wouldn't think twice. Is your life worth more than a one hundred dollar bill?"

"Yeah."

"Then prove it and do better than me."

"How can I do better than you, when you're the one driving a brand new Acura and wearing jewelry? I ride the bus."

"I know you see the flashy cars and jewelry, but I can lose it all in the blink of an eye and no one will care. You think these people that you see around me are my friends? They don't care about me and I don't care about them. It's kill or be killed and you don't have to deal with this. Your skills can take you to places far from poverty. You gotta bright future and you need to make sure you finish strong. What would your father say if he saw you down here?"

"I don't know my father," I replied.

Slim sat down next to me. "Neither did I, but you have a chance to be bigger than sitting on the block risking your life." Slim smiled showing his gold teeth. "If I had your skills, I would be practicing every night instead of sitting next to a lowlife like me. I know you think this is cool, but trust me – it's not. So don't look up to me, Keion. I want you to look beyond me."

I was stunned. I saw a different side of Slim and even though I was disappointed, I understood exactly what he was saying. If Slim didn't have my best interests, he could have easily used me like a pawn and paid me next to nothing to help him. All I wanted to do was be around him, but Slim took it upon himself to open my eyes. How many sons have fallen victim to the streets because they were infatuated with the danger? People aren't born to become drug dealers, it's a choice. For some, it's their circumstances, but for most, it's just a way to fit in. Boys will naturally gravitate to things that are masculine and without a father present most sons will make a mistake where the results are often death or prison.

Drug dealers are not bad people, they are simply misguided. Life is fragile and often based upon "what if" scenarios, but the power of an active father is greatly underestimated. If Slim's father was around, would that have kept Slim off the block? Who knows, but without a father the chances are greater and I was living proof.

> "I was so attached to Slim's lifestyle that I was willing to risk my freedom and my future just to be "down."
>
> -K. Carpenter

As I sat in shock from Slim's thoughtful, yet intellectual conversation, my mother's words replayed in my mind. She was right. She was always right and more than likely, she knew I was right here. She could've locked me in my room, but my mother knew that I would have just found another way. She knew I was curious and she took a chance by letting go of her overprotectiveness by allowing me to learn on my own.

I must reiterate this point to the mothers – you know your son better than he does, but if the father of your child is not present, there will come a time when you have to let your son burn himself. As long as you protect him, he will never know a flame exists. Is it a gamble? Of course it is, but this is the price we all pay from raising our children in broken homes. The term "broken" does not mean that you aren't doing your job. It simply means that your child is missing a vital part of becoming a responsible man. Being a man is your child's God given right, but becoming a responsible man often comes from making mistakes and learning from them. I wish there was one way to parenting, but as technology advances, our children are being exposed to the ways of the world at a pace that we can't fathom. Find a way to discipline, but give your child enough space to test your wisdom.

The obvious beauty in raising a child or children in a two-parent home is having two perspectives. In the "golden age" of parenting, typically, the father allowed the son to scrape his knee and the mother tended to the wound. With an absent father, who is allowing our sons to scrape their knee? A fatherless child is at a severe disadvantage and has been filling up jail cells and graveyards in record-breaking numbers. I had to make a decision if I was going to be an athlete or a drug dealer. And thanks to Slim, I didn't have a chance to decide. He made the choice for me. Had I lived in a two parent home or had an active father, the first time I was caught in the "hood" my dad would have made sure I saw the flipside of the flashy cars, girls, and jewelry.

The night sky was clear and it was time for me leave this hood fantasy and go back home to my reality. When I arrived home, I dropped my bag onto the

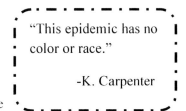

"This epidemic has no color or race."

-K. Carpenter

floor and my mother was sitting in the living room. I walked over to her and gave her a long hug. As she held me, I sank into her chest and I realized how blessed I was. This love I was feeling could not be duplicated. I thought about my actions and I felt guilt for going against her word. My mother didn't say much, as she didn't have to, but I could sense that she was happy to see me in one piece.

A few days later, I got the word that Slim was incarcerated for drug possession. I felt sorry for how his life ended, but I was relieved that I wasn't standing next to him when it happened. Slim knew that day was coming and we may not have been friends, but he liked me enough to keep me away. If Slim had not gone to prison, it was just a matter of time before I succumbed to his ways. God had other plans for me. Maybe removing Slim out of my life was God's way of putting me back on track.

Not too long after my friendship with Slim ended, my mother met a gentleman named William Harris, who later became my stepfather. Even though I respected him, I wasn't quite ready to give him the title as my father. While he tried his best to be the man that I needed, all I thought about was losing my mother. I did not have to impress him like my coaches and I was too young to understand that is what made him special. God sent Mr. William Harris to me even when I wasn't ready. My mother was very good at keeping her personal life away from me. I can only remember one relationship that did not turn out well and since then, I built a wall. Unfortunately, my stepfather had to climb it. Eventually, I realized how important he was to me and I love him for relentlessly trying to win my heart, even when I made it difficult. Spending time in the city exposed me to a lot and I believe Mr. Harris was sent to ease my transition back to my normal routine.

The summer vacation came to an end and old man winter was beginning to grin. Spending most of my summers in the "hood" changed me considerably. Seeing the other side of the world made me appreciate what I had. In the city, I played with kids who slept on the floor and barely had enough food in their fridge. Their home wasn't a place of refuge, but a trap and some of their mothers were too high on drugs to care. Before this experience, I was comfortable with hearing my name screamed from the crowd, but after this experience I wanted more than "hood" fame.

CHAPTER NINE

My last year of playing for the Woodlawn Recreational League had arrived, and I felt like I had done all I could do at this level. I was going to attend Woodlawn High, but I was a little intimidated since Woodlawn had the toughest team in Baltimore County. Besides the football program, I heard Woodlawn had the prettiest girls — and the rumor was true.

Most of my friends in my neighborhood also attended Woodlawn. My fame in the neighborhood followed me, but we all received the same treatment from the upperclassmen.

> "All the praise I received playing recreational football didn't mean a thing when I stepped onto Woodlawn's campus and I had to once again prove myself."
>
> -K. Carpenter

The minute you stepped onto Woodlawn's campus, you were forced to choose where you fit in. The cool kids congregated with the cool kids, the nerds congregated with the nerds, and the outcasts were rarely seen. I knew who I was when it came to sports, but without a father, I felt an enormous amount of pressure. I was no longer a virgin, but I had no clue how to approach girls and they were everywhere. Whenever an attractive girl looked my way, I dropped my head to avoid eye contact at all costs. Woodlawn High was a different world and it attracted different walks of life. In middle school, a teacher would stand in the hallway and direct traffic, but high school was much different. If you didn't know where you were going, you would find yourself wandering around the hallway.

I had my backpack strapped across my shoulders, while the upperclassmen and fully developed girls walked around with little to nothing in their hands. The hallways were crowded and everywhere I turned, someone was bumping up against me until I was in a daze. The bell rang and the crowded hallways turned into a ghost town and there I was still trying to find out what classroom I was supposed to report to. How come everyone knew where to go except for me? Was I dumb? While I stared at my piece of paper with my classroom number on it, I saw a group of guys running inside of the bathroom, but I pretended not to see them.

Once I finally found my classroom, I peeked inside and I immediately became nervous. I opened the door and all eyes were on me. I was used to receiving attention on the football field or on the basketball court, but this was different. I could feel everyone judging me from head to toe and my teacher made sure she used me as an example for arriving late.

"What's your name?" she asked looking at her clipboard.

For a few seconds I forgot, but I finally came to. "Keion Carpenter, ma'am."

"Well, don't just stand there. Find a seat," she sternly replied.

I scanned the classroom and inched my way to a seat in the back as far away from human contact as possible. I thought of all the men in my life, from my uncles to my coaches, and none of their words of encouragement could help me. Just when I thought I had life figured out, I once again needed my father. While my teacher handed out assignments, I wondered if my father even attended school. As I looked around at my classmates, most of them seemed to already know their purpose except for me. I was a bright kid, but this was the moment I realized that just being an athlete was not going to save me.

To the fathers who are reading this book, when your son was just a toddler, he wanted you, but your son was blessed to have a mother who took care of his needs. Now that your son is older, he becomes more complex and his needs change almost overnight. In this day in age, we as fathers cannot afford to send our sons into the world unprepared. Technology, social networks, and trending fads are changing faster than ever and it's much easier to get caught up. Think back to when you went to high school when you didn't have as much information at the tips of your fingers like the children today. With technology, the evils of the world are at their fingertips and if you are not there to help guide them, the outcome is your fault.

If you were blessed to have a son with extraordinary athletic ability, you should make it a necessity to keep that child on the right path because his mind is under attack every second of the day. Who's to blame when your son chooses to join a gang out of fear or simply because he wants to fit in? Who's to blame when your child experiments with drugs or erratic behavior? Blaming society and the school system is a thing of the past. Take responsibility for allowing your sons to fill up jail cells and caskets. Most children join gangs for protection, but if you're present, you are all the protection your son will ever need. How many stories must we watch on television or read in the newspapers of great young athletes destroying their future because of one bad decision? What makes you think your child is any different? As you know, the game of life never changes, only the faces and the names. If you continue to neglect your responsibility, you will become that grieving parent we see so often on television.

My first day at school was draining and when I arrived home, I collapsed onto the couch. In middle school, whenever I received homework assignments, my mother and I would sit down at the table, but those days were clearly over. To relieve my stress, I would walk to the basketball court and shoot around until I couldn't see the rim. I waited for my mother to scream my name, but it never came and that was when I realized I was responsible for how my life turned out. Things were changing, but since I didn't have my father, I still had the mindset of a child.

As the school year progressed, I made friends and I became a bit of a ladies man. Woodlawn High School was a very ruthless school and I witnessed some gruesome fights and altercations that led to wars between neighborhoods. During this time, I saw my neighborhood, Campfield, go through many changes and the place where I once found peace became a haven for crime and drugs. Whenever life got the best of me, the basketball court was my refuge and now I had to look over my shoulder. In the past, I would go into the city to experience these things, but now, it was around the corner.

One afternoon, I was playing basketball with my friends and it was no longer about fun. Competitions would often lead to fights or even shootings that would clear the basketball court for days. During this time, becoming a hustler was another way of becoming a man. The city life, and the city life mindset, pushed its way into the county and I watched my childhood friends become drug dealers. In the past, all we needed was a basketball, but I began to see guns and knots of money inside of gym bags.

"My conversation with Slim kept me from indulging in the drug game, but it was very enticing."

-K. Carpenter

Being a great basketball player in my neighborhood kept me in the middle of a lot of drama, and some of the older kids who attended Woodlawn High School took a liking to me. The company I kept was labeled as "trouble makers," but they were my friends. We had a special unbreakable bond and we protected each other. I soon established myself at Woodlawn High School and I stood out from most freshmen. In the cafeteria, I sat with the who's who and it felt good to be accepted by them and treated as their equal. Soon, the gang mentality became very relevant in the hallways of Woodlawn High School and certain neighborhoods would turn the simplest disagreement into an all−out war. Even though I received a lot of respect for my athletic abilities, things changed when I showed my friends I wasn't afraid to fight.

When it came to my neighborhood, we stood up for each other and we often found ourselves sitting in the principal's office facing suspension. I was slowly becoming just like my friends and I knew my grandfather noticed. My grandfather's approach was always calculated. He never bombarded me with questions, but he always knew how to get the answers he needed.

One afternoon, I walked into the house and my grandfather noticed I didn't have my book bag. Before I could go upstairs, he calmly called me over to sit down next to him. Before he spoke, he just stared at me and I anxiously tapped the heel of my shoe against the floor. As we sat in absolute silence, I thought about everything I did wrong that could have gotten back to him. He sat up, and gave me "the look" that only he could give and said, "I know you're becoming a man, Keion, but only you can save you from making the wrong decision. We can't chase after you anymore. I see some of the people you are hanging out with and I used to be just like you. Boys will be boys, but it's time for you to start thinking like a man." My grandfather adjusted himself in his seat. "Your mother has worked very hard to give you all that she can, so don't disappoint her."

When my grandfather spoke, I knew he meant well, but I was so naïve and immature that I didn't take heed to his advice. "What about my father?" I asked. "How come he hasn't taken the time to make sure that I'm okay? If he doesn't care, why should I?"

"Only your father can explain that to you, Keion, but you can't use that as a crutch to not care about your own life. You know how you can fix that?" he asked.

My eyes grew wide. "How?"

"You can make sure that you never let your children feel what you feel."

When my grandfather gave me this advice, he was so far into my future that it wasn't helpful until I had my first child. My grandfather was always light years ahead of me, but that still didn't help me deal with the pressure I felt when I stepped outside of my home. Before I left, my grandfather had a few more words.

"Everyone knows that you are a talented athlete, and every time I hear a gunshot, I pray to God that you aren't on the receiving end. Do you believe that you are extraordinary?"

"Yes."

"Then don't do anything that will jeopardize it."

When I closed the front door behind me, I saw some of my friends on the corner and that was my moment to take my grandfathers advice. I didn't.

As a young teenage man, I convinced myself that my grandfather couldn't understand me, but in reality, he knew me

> "It's not that my grandfather's advice wasn't useful, it just didn't come from my father."
>
> -K Carpenter

better than I knew myself. I was beginning to spend more time on the corner with my friends than perfecting my skills. My freshman year, we spent our days hunting down the girls in my neighborhood and we were often successful to say the least. We felt invincible and unprotected sex was the norm. The sounds of 2 Pac, Naughty By Nature, Pete Rock & C.L. Smooth, Ice Cube, Ghetto Boys, Nas, and A Tribe Called Quest became the soundtracks to our lives. We were a bunch of fatherless children trying to mimic our role models and our bellies were filled with cheap malt liquor and weed. There I was, a future National Football League player risking it all for a night out on the town.

I could have lost it all, but those experiences helped me become a man. If I had an active father, would I have still done stupid things to fit in? Probably so, but I would have known when to stop. Everyone I surrounded myself with wasn't my friend and I found myself in situations only God could save me from. Most of the trouble I got into never reached my mother mainly because my grandfather shielded me from her wrath. He never forced his opinion on me, but always said just enough for me to remember.

> ### Coaches Corner
>
> We will all make bad decisions as a child and even into adulthood, but if we are not able to find the lesson from that bad decision, we'll just become repeat offenders.

One evening, I sat outside with my friends while they shot dice and smoked weed in the open as if it were legal. I was never much of a gambler, but I was addicted to the excitement. As they shot dice, I saw a gun on the hip of one of my close friends and to protect his identity, I'll call him Samuel. Samuel was a fatherless child just like I was, except he wasn't much of an athlete or a scholar in school. Samuel's father was incarcerated and ever since he was a child, Samuel had to visit his father from inside of the penitentiary walls. Samuel was a good person, but every day of his life, the person he admired was a criminal so getting into trouble seemed to be the only way he could relate to his father.

Over time, Samuel became a full time hustler which led to becoming a well-known "stickup kid," but his friends were always exempt from his reckless behavior. Samuel spoke a lot about his father. He wore his father's name and reputation like a badge of honor, but with that honor came pressure to uphold his name. Samuel spoke about his father's drug dealing and gun toting ways as if his father graduated from Morehouse, I could still see the pain and emptiness he felt.

When I was younger, I envied my friends who got the opportunity to speak to or see their father, but as I got older, I no longer envied them and I found comfort in not knowing my father at all. Ever since my mother dragged me up those courthouse steps, I knew that lifestyle was not for me. I often wondered if the impact of seeing your father in jail was better or worse than seeing your father at all. Samuel would later prove that it was worse.

On this particular night, there were hundreds of dollars on the ground and the atmosphere was extremely tense. The dice game didn't begin until five in the afternoon and it lasted until almost eleven o'clock at night. As each hour passed, I watched the dice game go from an innocent game amongst friends, to a treacherous mindset of winning it all. Samuel rolled the dice and the second they left his hand, I knew it wasn't going to end well. He lost over five hundred dollars and I watched his face turn from a smile to a look of despair. Without a second thought, Samuel, my friend that I've known since middle school pulled out his gun and everyone froze.

"I can't let you take that money," he said.

My grandfather's words rang in my head like an alarm, but I never thought my childhood friend would be the one holding the weapon. *This can't be happening.* Time slowed up, he looked at me and his face was filled with guilt, but that didn't stop him. I could feel my heart pounding through my chest and I was afraid to speak.

He not only took the money off the floor, he walked over to me and said, "Gimme whatchu got."

I reached into my pocket and all I had was three dollars. He snatched it out of my hand as if he never knew me and treated everyone else the same before running off. After being robbed by one of my closest friends, my trust was shattered. We were a bunch of kids raised in single-family homes. Without a father to help guide our paths, some of my friends went off course and it often led to destruction.

To the fathers who are incarcerated, I am not saying that your incarceration will spiral your son down a path of destruction. What I want to make clear is if your son's superhero is behind bars, the chances of him spending time in an orange jumpsuit are higher. A caring father who is incarcerated uses that opportunity to show their sons the outcome of bad decisions. But we all know, once those visiting hours are over, your son becomes property of the street. Make every visit, call, or letter count.

★★★

Later that night, I lay in my bed clueless. I was robbed by my friend, and I had to go to school and pretend like nothing happened. With little to no sleep, my alarm clock sounded at 7 o'clock in the morning. I wanted to play sick, but I knew my mother wouldn't buy it. After getting dressed and trying my best to miss my bus, I walked downstairs and my grandfather called me over.

"Are you okay?" he asks.

I just nodded my head, but inside I was terrified.

My grandfather looked me in the eyes and said, "We'll always be here for you, Keion, but every day is the first day of your life and you only get one time to get it right."

This time, my grandfather's words hit me like a ton of bricks. It was as if he knew exactly what I felt. From that point, I intended on being very careful with whom I allowed into my circle, but peer pressure was almost unavoidable. I sat in my math class bored out of my mind when I saw one of my friends in the hallway. Terrance was another product of a fatherless home and school was his playground. Terrance always reeked of marijuana and to this day, I wonder how he graduated. He stood in the doorway of the classroom, reached beneath his shirt, and pulled out a bottle of "Mad dog 20/20." As I watched Terrance holding this glass bottle containing eighteen percent alcohol, my grandfather's words once again sounded off like an alarm. But, my curiosity and urge to fit in was much more powerful.

Seconds later, the bell rang dismissing my class and the hallways were once again filled with chaos. Terrance had this mischievous aura around him and everyone loved the "bad guy." I followed Terrance out the back door and walked to the bridge. I had heard many stories about "the bridge" and they were all true. I saw a group of people hanging at "the bridge" smoking and drinking without fear. Terrance twisted off the cap and the smell of trouble tingled my nose.

> "I knew everything that I was doing was taking me away from my goal, but I couldn't stop. None of us could."
>
> -K. Carpenter

I stumbled back to the school with the smell of alcohol seeping through my pores. My eyes were glassy and there was something exciting about hearing my classmates talk about my alcohol stained breath. To the older students, I was "down" and to the girls, I was a "bad boy." I loved the attention even though it was destructive behavior to my ultimate goal.

I sat in my next class trying to look sober when I heard the worst possible news ever. My Principle's voice blasted over the intercom. *"Attention students, basketball tryouts will begin today. If you're interested, please report to the gymnasium immediately after school."* My heart stopped. The moment I had been waiting for had finally arrived, yet my breath smelled like Mad dog 20/20, and I could barely keep my eyes open. I immediately felt shame because my grandfather warned me of my one shot and I may have already ruined it. The bell rang dismissing me from class, so I dodged through the crowded hallway, sped by Terrance, and pushed open the bathroom doors. I splashed water over my face in an attempt to sober up, but all that did was leave a huge wet mark on the front of my shirt. I panicked and the sound of my grandfather's voice haunted me. While staring at my reflection in the stained bathroom mirror, Terrance walked in holding a half empty bottle of Mad dog 20/20.

"Why'd you run by me? And why are you splashing water over your face?"

"I gotta try out for the basketball team, and I'm trying to sober up."

Terrance laughed so hard he clutched his stomach. "But, you're a freshman! You're not gonna make the team, so one more sip won't hurt," he said pushing the bottle in my face.

As peer pressure presented itself yet again, I stared at Terrance and a moment of clarity came over me. Now that I'm older, I realized that I was being tested. Terrance was just being himself. He never forced me to indulge; he simply provided the opportunity. As parents, we must realize that our children are not being forced; they are making decisions. That was another pivotal moment in my life; I could have chosen to take another sip of Mad dog 20/20 or pursue my goal.

"Nah, I'm cool."

I expected Terrance to make fun of me, but instead, he placed the bottle back into his jeans and left. Before that moment, I was afraid to risk fitting in I didn't realize the power of the word "no" and it felt good to do what was best for me. I was still slightly buzzed, but nothing was going to stop me from getting a spot on the basketball team. With a damp shirt, I walked into the gymnasium, and an overwhelming focus came over me. I made a name for myself on neighborhood basketball courts all over Baltimore City, but playing for a school was the ultimate test. I walked inside and instantly realized that I was the smallest in the gym, but where I lacked in size, I made up in heart. Playing "street−ball" taught me how to be fearless, but it did not teach me the fundamentals of the game.

There are no refs or coaches in "street−ball," just skill and the will to win. My neighborhood reputation preceded itself and the coaches at Woodlawn High School were eager to see if I could live up to the hype. As I ran up and down the court, I could feel the effects of Mad dog 20/20 taking a toll on my body. I was fatigued, I sweated profusely, and I felt a slight migraine on the right side of my brain. I was being outplayed by people who were not better than me. With every shot I missed, I felt my opportunity slipping away. My plan was to make the varsity team, but after my performance I would be lucky to play at all. The first day of tryouts ended and I sat on the bleachers with my face buried in my arms. All of a sudden, my mouth began to water. I ran to the bathroom, fell to my knees and vomited. Ironically, I felt better, but it was too late. I had no one to blame. I was forced to deal with my decision to fit in, and those individuals I tried to impress were not there to pick me up and give me words of encouragement when I needed it the most.

The very next day, I went to school and I made sure I stayed away from anything and anyone that would get in my way. Terrance was still being Terrance, but it was time for me to be myself. The bell rang dismissing me from my last class and I headed straight to the gymnasium for tryouts. As soon as I stepped onto the basketball court, I showed everyone that I could play at a high level. My mission was to live up to the hype and I exceeded that goal and earned my spot on the Junior Varsity team.

Since childhood, I enjoyed hearing people scream my name after a big play, but I was not given the chance during my freshman year. I spent most of my time on the sideline cheerleading and it killed me on the inside. It was a very humbling experience and it taught me patience, which was something I knew nothing about. Even though I was learning this valuable lesson, I felt like a disappointment. There I was, the best player in my neighborhood and I wasn't even starting on my team.

CHAPTER TEN

The year was 1993. I was set to begin the tenth grade, and it was time for me to claim my spot. After a lackluster freshman year, I trained extra hard during the summer to sharpen my skills. Before the basketball season began, the junior varsity and varsity coaches held a few open gyms to scout the talent. I didn't care who was in front of me. It was never personal, all business — and after the whistle, I would gladly shake hands and congratulate my opponents. But until I heard that whistle, my plan was to destroy you and I often did. I played so hard and with so much determination that the basketball varsity coach told me to try out for the varsity team. All summer, I waited to hear those words, but I had a decision to make. Should I stay at the junior varsity level and outscore my opponents or make the varsity team and sit on the bench?

Yet again, another moment where I wished my father was a part of my life. Even if my mind was already made, I would have loved to have this one—on—one conversation with my father. My competitive nature would not allow me to just dominate at the junior varsity level, so I tried for a starting spot on the varsity team. I was no longer intrigued with trying to fit in, but I couldn't say the same for my friends. They were becoming men and violence became more prevalent. Those who used drugs saw it becoming a business and the term "hustling" took the neighborhood by storm. It divided Baltimore County into sections, and teenagers became territorial watchdogs. These same childhood friends who I grew up with became enemies overnight simply because they lived a few blocks away, and I was often caught in the middle.

One of the most notable "beefs" that took place was between those who lived in Cross Creek and my neighborhood, Campfield.

Whenever my bus pulled up to the front of the school, I could feel the tension. Something was bound to happen and everyone knew it. As I walked towards the school, I saw a group of guys from Cross Creek standing in the distance and one of my teammates was with them. I'll call him John. John was a year older than I was and he was a pretty decent player. John and I built our relationship on the basketball court, but the John who I saw standing in the middle of this rowdy group of teenagers was not my teammate. As my neighborhood friends walked behind me, I could feel the situation intensifying and I knew my sophomore year was going to be difficult. John and I were in the same predicament; we were caught between being loyal to our neighborhood versus honoring each other as teammates. Thankfully, nothing happened.

Later that day, I met John at the gymnasium and there was an awkward silence. During practice, we were not separated by the actions of our friends. After practice, I walked into the locker room and John was sitting on the bench in deep thought. I sat down next to him and asked, "How are we supposed to be on the same team and our neighborhoods hate each other?" I hoped that John would have an answer, but he was just as confused as I was. We sat next to each other in silence. For John and I, playing basketball was bigger than winning. It was our way to escape what we faced every day and we were allowing our outside influences to affect our goals. John and I had more in common than just basketball; we also didn't have active fathers in our lives.

> "During this time of ignorance, God had us all covered."
>
> -K. Carpenter

For months, Woodlawn High School was plagued with violence which often led to gun shots on both sides. John and I were in a position to end this war of differences, but we weren't equipped with the knowledge from our fathers to settle our differences. The children of today are missing this quality and it's causing the death of too many.

At any moment, my career could have been cut short from a bullet or stab wound. Even though I wasn't the one starting the trouble, I didn't provide a solution.

The year 1993 did not get off to a good start, but I was willing to change that through sports. It wasn't intentional, but John and I were only seen with each other on the basketball court. We were afraid to show our relationship off the basketball court in fear that our friends would label us as "punks", but one afternoon, I decided to become the leader that I am today.

I walked inside of the crowded cafeteria and it was oddly quiet. After numerous fights, the teaching staff was spread throughout the cafeteria expecting the worst to happen. My neighborhood friends were sitting to the left and no one was eating. Instead, they were staring down the Cross Creek crew ready to prove their loyalty. I saw John standing in the lunch line, so instead of sitting with my neighborhood, I stood behind John and mumbled, "We should sit together." John gave me a look of bafflement, but I didn't care.

"What about your friends?" John asked.

"Aren't we friends?"

"Yeah."

"Don't friends sit together?"

"Yeah."

"We can change this; we have to at least try."

John was hesitant, but he knew I was right. He found an empty table in the distance and I followed behind him. I could hear the whispers from both sides but I refused to make eye contact with my friends. We sat down and all eyes were on us. This moment not only showed both sides that we could get along, it proved it. What John and I did, didn't stop all the violence between our neighborhoods, but it planted a seed and through sports, we were able to make a stance for what was right. Some of my friends didn't understand my decision and some called me a "sellout," but I was willing to deal with the backlash for the greater good. These moments helped me to become responsible. To this day, I wonder if I would have found a resolution sooner if I had a father figure in my life. I'll never know, but to those dads who are active in their children's lives you can teach them the importance of resolving issues and you can start with your relationship with the mother of your child.

★★★

At Woodlawn High School, I established myself as a two-sport athlete. I was the starting quarterback for the junior varsity team, but on the varsity basketball team I barely played. After weeks of sitting on the bench, my coach finally gave me the opportunity. I was determined to get the same respect I received on the football field, and I finally did. I had to beat out three point guards for the starting spot and the odds were against me. The competition was high, but God had a plan for me and it is the same plan that God has for your child. As a parent, it is your job to equip your child with the discipline to trust God and meet Him halfway.

The upperclassmen knew I was gunning for their spot and midway through the season, I earned the starting point guard position on the varsity basketball team. I was the youngest and I wore the leadership tag like a badge of honor. All I wanted to do was put in work. I was never afraid of pushing myself to the max and once I reached the max, I pushed some more. In my non–professional and professional career, I've seen many athletes try to take short cuts when it comes to hard work and they often fell short.

You may be bigger and better than I am, but you will never out work me. I never quit at anything and I adopted this attitude ever since I was seven years old. When I was given the starting point guard position on the varsity team, everything changed. I remember hearing the crowd scream my name when I was just a little guy trying to impress my mother, but the energy I felt inside of the Woodlawn High School gymnasium was electrifying. Every junior varsity player wanted to play on the varsity team. I inspired them to believe that anything was possible with hard work. When I meet young men who grew up in a fatherless household, I understand their fears and insecurities, but I refused to

110

pacify them. I was just like them and I faced the same obstacles they did, so I know that each child possesses that fire to achieve far beyond their wildest dreams. To achieve this without a father is very difficult, but I am proof that it can be done.

The more my performance on the basketball court became the talk of the town, the more I felt people rooting for me. Teachers and students that wouldn't even look my way a season ago would now pat me on the back and give me words of encouragement. When I was young, all I wanted to do was make my mother happy, but that changed considerably in High School. That chip I carried on my shoulder since I was four years old was beginning to fade. I finally felt like I had nothing to prove and everything to prove all at the same time. Ironically, my father's disappearing act helped me to reach higher heights as a person.

They say it takes a village to raise a child and this was my Woodlawn Village: Mr. Erik King, Mr. Russell, Mr. Eric Carlton, Ms. Inez Butler, and most of all Mr. Brian Scriven. I couldn't get away with anything in school without them knowing about it. They were all on the same team and they each played different positions in my life. Mr. King reiterated that I was "special" and only I could prevent God's plan. Mr. Carlton cared about my well−being. Our conversations were more about life, choices, and the decisions I was making. At times, it was hard for me to determine who cared about me or who only cared about my athletic abilities. Mr. Carlton showed me that he was far more concerned with how my life turned out.

Mr. Brian Scriven was like my father. He was the one who would snatch me up by the collar in front of anyone. At times, it was embarrassing, but he knew I had the ability to go to a division one college and the last thing I needed was a smudge on my school record. I dominated my tenth grade year and I was beginning to get recognition in the daily newspaper. I wondered if the local news article reached my father and he was watching me from a distance. As a star athlete, I spent most of my time on getting better. I was obsessed with proving everyone wrong even when there wasn't anyone left. Or, was there?

I began receiving letters from colleges and I can remember the first letter like it was yesterday. I was beyond excited because my football future was beginning to form right before my eyes. I was just in the tenth grade, so was this really happening? How could all of these colleges see something in me, while my father closed his eyes? The sporadic pain I felt was similar to losing someone to death.

I spent most of my days not thinking about my father, but every now and again, I would feel this uncontrollable sorrow that would turn a perfectly happy teenager into a depressed, closed off child. I despised my father for forcing me to deal with this question mark that burned inside the pit of my stomach. A piece of my happiness was taken and every recruitment letter I received made me think about my father.

112

In my junior year, I was ranked in the top 100 players from the eastern region in the country and the feeling was indescribable. I dreamed of being recognized by my peers, but deep down I knew that the more my name was echoed the chances of my father and I reconnecting would increase. One Wednesday evening, I sat in the kitchen with my books spread across the table when my mother showed me a sealed letter from Boston College. My eyes grew wide and for a split second, the world came to a complete halt. I dropped my pen, closed my notebook, and stared.

"Aren't you going to say something?" my mother asked with the biggest smile on her face that my teenage eyes had seen.

I anxiously looked over the letter and ran my fingers across the Boston College logo. The moment was unreal. Even though I was sitting in my mother's small kitchen, in my mind I was standing on the Boston College fifty−yard line. The stands were filled with thousands of students waving banners and screaming my name at the top of their lungs. I had no clue how the recruitment process worked, but I knew if I was getting mail from Boston College as a junior − the bidding war for my athletic ability was promising. After reading a few lines of the acceptance letter, I realized that it wasn't a scholarship, but an unofficial invitation to their camp. My excitement turned into anxiety and a fear came over me. *Am I really good enough to compete with the best of the best?* All the cheers and accolades didn't matter anymore because now I had to show−and−prove. This was another moment that marked itself in history that I didn't share with my father.

My mother leaned up against the wall and asked again, "Aren't you going to say something?"

"Yeah, where's Boston College?"

"You know the coaches name, the stats, and the names of all the starters, but you don't know where Boston College is?" she said laughing. "It's in Massachusetts."

"That's sounds far, Ma."

"It is."

"Are you going with me?"

I transformed back into my mother's little boy right before her eyes. She unfolded her arms, kneeled down and placed her hands on my face. "No, baby, you're going alone."

"Alone?"

"You'll only be gone for three days, Keion. What's wrong? Isn't this the school of your dreams?"

For years, I bottled up these feelings of emptiness. I wasn't comfortable with traveling to Boston College, but what bothered me more was not having my father there. I never wanted my mother to feel underappreciated, but my heart wouldn't allow me to remain quiet. I looked my mother in her eyes and asked, "Do you think my father will ever show up?"

"I don't want to lie to you, Keion. I don't know."

"How come everyone recognizes me except him? He's my father!"

I saw my mother looking for the right words. She saw my pain and confusion, but all she could do was stare. After an awkward silence, she inched closer to me and said, "Your father loves you. He just doesn't know how to express it. You have become a great young man, Keion, so don't let this frustrate you. I want you to go to Boston College and show them what you're made of. Okay?"

I had never been outside of Baltimore, Maryland and I was terrified. I was accustomed to having my friends, my coaches and my corner, but the tide was changing. The day before my trip to Boston College, my appetite was nonexistent and I could barely sleep.

Whenever I watched Boston College play football on television, they appeared to be like giants with unbelievable speed. Wearing boxers and no shirt, I stood in front of my bedroom mirror and stared at my reflection. I clinched my fists and gritted my teeth, but the words that echoed in my mind were, "I can't do this." My spirit was under attack and I needed God to step in. With my stomach in knots, I fell to my knees and prayed. My relationship with God was pretty strong for a teenager. I didn't quite know how to serve God, but I knew the connection I felt was real. My unwavering dedication to my Lord and Savior gave me the peace I needed at that moment.

> "My skills were taking me to places that no one could go, not even my father. This type of 'alone' was new to me and it became another challenge that I had to face."
>
> -K. Carpenter

That night, I taped Boston College's letter on my mirror. I received many letters but this was the first letter I received from a college in the Big Eastern Conference. Most of Boston College's games were televised, which meant if I was accepted, I would be that much closer to the National Football League. As I waited for the day to travel to Boston College, my mother continued to keep me calm and give me words of encouragement. I appreciated her, but I needed my father. I didn't care if my dad was a football guru or if he did not the know the difference between a running back and a quarterback. I simply needed him to sit next to me, place his arm around my shoulder and go on this emotional journey with me. How many times did I need to be reminded that he wasn't present? I didn't realize until I was an adult that this feeling would remain until we stood face to face. Every day that passed, my trip to Boston College was drawing near, but more importantly, this was my first trip outside of Baltimore.

My alarm rang at 7:45 in the morning and I sprang out of bed. The last time I felt like this, was my first game as a toddler. I once again had to prove myself, but this time, one mistake could determine my future. The pressure was unbelievable and my stomach was doing cartwheels. I still remember the prayer I said before leaving my room. I fell to my knees and closed my eyes. "Dear, Lord. I don't know why you chose me, but I'm grateful. I don't know what to expect, but I ask that you guide me every step of the way, Amen." After my brief conversation with God, a burst of energy came over me. My trust with God was getting stronger, and I knew I could call on Him when all else failed.

God doesn't have an age requirement; He will meet you wherever you are, and He met me in my small bedroom. I encourage all parents to help their children build a relationship with God. As parents, we will not always know how to reach our children and we have to teach them to go to God when they feel like no one will understand.

116

Fully dressed, I ran downstairs and waited by the window for Coach Scriven to arrive. Minutes later, my mother walked downstairs rubbing her eyes.

"You'll do fine," she said before giving me a long hug.

"I know."

"That's what I wanted to hear, Keion."

Coach Scriven honked the horn. I looked at my mother one last time, grabbed my bag, and headed out. As we drove to the bus station, I bombarded him with questions, and all he said was to "stay focused." We arrived at the bus station and reality hit me like a ton of bricks. I realized that the moment I stepped out of Coach Scriven's car, I was on my own. With a bus ticket in my hand and my bags over my shoulder, I gave Coach Scriven a hug and took my first step into adulthood. Seventeen hours later, I arrived at Boston College where I saw a large group of athletes who received the same invitation I did. Those guys were the best of the best and I wasn't going to leave there without making my mark.

I could feel everyone sizing each other up. The atmosphere was friendly and relaxed, but each one of us knew that as soon as that whistle blew, it was all about conquering your opponent. I couldn't believe I was standing in front of the same school I had watched on television for years. A week ago, I was running my fingers across Boston College's logo on my invitation letter and here I was. For years, I debated if I wanted to play basketball or football, but this moment was a clear deciding factor. Playing basketball had taken me to basketball courts all over the city, but football had opened up my eyes to a much bigger world. I wished my friends could experience this, but the reality was most would never get a chance at a higher education.

One of the coaches blew their whistle. He was a very tall, militant man and wasted no time with letting everyone know that we were privileged to be there. We may have been the best in our schools, region, or country – but we were a bunch of nobody's at Boston College. They escorted us down to the field and I never felt so small in my life. The stadium sat forty–four thousand five hundred people and was very intimidating. I envisioned myself running onto the field in front of thousands of fans and my will to be the best would not be denied. Once we began our drills, my nervousness disappeared and I was more than ready to perform. Even though I had been a quarterback, the coaches at Boston College clearly had a different position for me in mind. They didn't care about my stats or reputation; they were looking for heart and determination. Whenever my name was called, I rose to the occasion and I impressed the coaches on the first day of training. On the second day of training, I realized that I wasn't just playing with the best – I was earning my respect.

On the last day of training, one of the coaches approached me after practice with a huge smile on his face. "Mr. Carpenter, you're going to have a bright future," he said standing over me with his arms folded.

"Thank you, coach."

"We could use someone like you in our secondary. You have a nose for the ball and you play with great intellect."

I couldn't believe a coach from Boston College took the time to speak to me. Since I arrived, all they did was yell, blow their whistles, and give out orders. I tried to stay composed, but on the inside I was jumping up down from excitement. I was living my dream and I would not take this for granted.

"Keion, would you like to play for Boston College?"

"Yes, sir!"

"Good. Keep your grades up and make sure you have an outstanding senior year," he replied before walking off and approaching another prospect.

I'm sure he gave this same pep talk to the next guy, but I didn't care. I was in the eleventh grade and I competed with seniors who were bigger and faster, and I made an impact. I left my heart on Boston College's football field and I knew they would be watching me for the rest of my high school career. After the last day of training, I sat in my dorm room with a highly recruited player from San Antonio, Texas. Benjamin was a three hundred and seventy-five pound giant. He was a senior and clearly going to the National Football League.

When I first met Benjamin, I wasn't sure how a black guy from Baltimore and a Caucasian giant from Texas would get along, but we had something in common other than our love for football. After a brief conversation, I learned that Benjamin's parents divorced when he was eleven years old, and the last memory he had was watching his father storm out of the house. This huge man who was an undeniable force on the football field had a weakness; he was fatherless. Even though my time with Benjamin was short, he taught me a very valuable lesson.

On the last day, Benjamin and I shared stories of our childhood and it seemed the absence of his father had a much deeper impact than mine. Unfortunately, in the black community, it wasn't uncommon to be raised in a single family home, but in Benjamin's world this type of rejection was much deeper.

During this seventeen–hour trip to Boston College, I created a bond with Benjamin and players from all over the world. My visit to Boston College changed my life. I learned to think more independently and my confidence was at an all–time high. Even though this was an unofficial visit to Boston College, I was ready to sign my name on the dotted line. Little did I know, my visit at Boston College would peek the interest of other top colleges across the country. My football future was just beginning.

"I conditioned myself to believe that a fatherless child was a 'black thing', but I was clearly wrong."

K. Carpenter

CHAPTER ELEVEN

"If I could go back in time, I would tell each of my friends,
"don't worry, you'll do just fine."

—K. Carpenter

In my opinion, when men lack fathers, the bond that is created with their friends is priceless. During my childhood and teenage years, I made many friends, but only a few helped me grow as a man. We were all individuals, but our personalities came together like the perfect puzzle. No matter how much praise I received in sports, my friends always treated me like them, and I needed that. We didn't always do the right thing, but we always did them together. I grew up not having any blood brothers, but God surrounded me with love. We spent countless hours and days together enjoying our youth, playing sports, and of course I can't forget about the women. I would do anything for those guys and the favor was always returned. They helped me stay focused and they often reminded me that I was going to be the "ticket out of the hood."

My friends had more in common than running the halls at Woodlawn High School. We were all athletes raised in fatherless homes except for Neville Jr. Neville Hodge Jr. was born in St. Croix and later moved to Baltimore to live with his father. Neville Jr. was a fast talker by nature who possessed an attitude that I connected with. Neville Hodge Sr., was a three–time Olympian for the US Virgin Islands. He was also an eight–time NCAA All American, and the current World Record Holder in the 100–meter dash. Neville Hodge Jr. had an active father, but because of his father's career the emptiness he felt was similar to mine.

Neville Jr. followed in his father's footsteps and became a track star at Woodlawn High School. He made his father proud and he had the relationship we all envied. When I first met Neville Jr. and his father, I was jealous. While the rest of our mothers made sure there was dinner on the table, Neville Jr. had to wash his clothes and cook for himself. His father loved him dearly, but the way a father raises their son is completely different from a mother. Neville Jr. may not have received the soft kisses on the forehead or a long hug, but he learned to become independent at an early age.

"I was always intrigued by Neville's relationship with his father. Now that I look back, I can see the difference. He learned the harshness of life and he knew how to handle situations that most of us were unaware of. A lesson taught by a father that will last a lifetime."

—K. Carpenter

★★★

All of our parents did their best, but we raised each other during these pivotal years. Whatever void there was, we filled it the best way we could by simply having unconditional love for each other. I also had a female "crew" that made sure I stayed on the right path. They treated me like their brother and they made sure I was protected from those 'hot' girls who wanted nothing but to be associated with a star athlete. I was blessed to have those types of people in my corner. They genuinely loved me and wanted nothing more than to see me where I ultimately ended up, which was playing sports at a professional level. I've seen many men reach levels of success, acquire new friends, and lose sight of those who helped them along the way. I'm honored and proud to say that these people are still in my life today. It took an entire school, friends, and family to fill the void of my father — but I was covered.

The year was 1995, and I was a senior. The basketball season ended and football season was set to begin. I was beyond ready and everyone knew it. All I had to do was keep my grades in good standing and stay out of trouble, which wasn't always easy. I was Keion Carpenter, star athlete at Woodlawn High School, and the bleachers were filled with scouts. Even though I was the quarterback, I rarely stepped off the field. I played multiple positions and I was naturally a ball hawk. Since I was a toddler, I always believed that I had what it took. I was reminded every time I saw a college scout in the bleachers. Inside the hallways of Woodlawn High School was a glass case with Carlton Bailey's jersey hanging inside. During my freshmen and sophomore years, I would give the glass case a glance, but my senior year was the year that I envisioned my very own jersey on display.

One afternoon, I was called into the principal's office. As I walked down the hallway, I thought about anything wrong that I did to warrant this request. I walked inside of the principal's office and sat down. My principal reached under his desk and pulled out a basket of acceptance letters to multiple colleges.

"What are you going to do, Keion?" he asked.

I visited Boston College, NC State, Wisconsin, and Virginia Tech and this question haunted me at night. My father was once again not present. My mother tried her best and I loved her for it, but what I needed was my Alpha Male to help me decide. When I was a child, my mother told me she could not afford to put me in college. My grades were okay, but it didn't take a rocket scientist to realize that my ticket to a higher education would come from my athletic ability. As I sat in my principal's office looking for the right words to say, he continued to comb through my acceptance letters.

"So what's it going to be?"

"I don't know."

"Many children don't get the opportunity that you have, Keion, and I don't want you to ruin it."

"I won't."

"Are you sure about that? At some point, you're going to have to realize that you cannot continue to do the same things."

"What do you mean?"

"The company that you keep can cause you to lose it all."

"My friends wouldn't do anything to hurt me."

"I'm sure they won't, but their actions will. You can have a bright future, but only you can determine your fate."

As my principal continued to give me the lecture from hell, I just nodded my head in agreement. I'm not sure what caused him to hold this meeting, but he couldn't have been more right. About a month or so after my meeting with my principal, a friend of mine got into an altercation with a rival neighborhood. The days of ending differences with your fists were coming to an end and a simple altercation could lead to gunfire. One Thursday evening, I heard four hard knocks at my door. I answered and my friend had a look of revenge in his face.

"Yo, we about get'em tonight. We know where they are, you coming?"

Behind my friend was a car filled with people ready to seek revenge and they stared at me. Time seemed to slow down and my principal's words echoed in my head. My friends would die for me and even though I knew I was getting in over my head, I couldn't tell them no. Within a matter of seconds, I was riding in the back of my friends gray station wagon. They passed a bottle of Thunder Bird back and forth when one of my friends passed me a black nine—millimeter. I had seen a gun before, but I never held one in my hand.

> "The advantage I had over my opponents on the football field and the basketball court couldn't compare to the power this weapon gave me."
>
> -K. Carpenter

As my friends drove, I could hear this faint whisper, *What are you doing, Keion?* I was a top recruit with a full scholarship to the college of my choice and I was riding around with a gun in my hand. The power of this weapon was too much for me to handle, so I gave it back. I was always down to put up my fists and fight, but taking someone's life — my God just wouldn't allow.

My friend turned down the music. "That's them right there," he said gritting his teeth. The driver slowed the car down, parked in the distance, and we all got out. The closer we got, the more afraid I became. I wasn't afraid of being physically hurt, I was afraid that this night was going to ruin my future. We inched closer and I watched one of my friends raise his gun and open fire. I had watched many movies like this, but nothing could compare to the real thing. Each time I heard a gunshot, I wondered if that was the bullet that killed someone. We didn't stick around to find out. I ran back to the car, and my heart pounded so hard that I could hear it through my chest. I never ran this fast in my life. My friend drove frantically through the city until we arrived at my house. I jumped out of the car and didn't look back. Once I got inside, I fell onto my bed and buried my face into my pillow. Moments later, I fell to my knees and prayed that no one was on the receiving end of those bullets. I thank God that my prayers were answered.

Later that evening, my mother walked into my room and she could tell something was wrong, but I wasn't going to say a word. I knew she would overreact, so I had to once again deal with a life—changing event without my father. Now that I have sons and I dealt with these types of situations without a father, I know how I would respond. I would share my stories and let them know that they will always have the option to not participate. I will share with my son the power in the word "no" and explain that it is okay to have friends, but it is also okay to have limitations. I knew my mother couldn't provide the comfort that I needed. That night changed my life and I made a conscious decision to remove myself from negativity even if it came from my close friends.

How many times have you read or watched these types of stories unfold, when an extraordinary athlete loses it all because he was in the wrong place at the wrong time or made a conscious decision to do so? How many sons have fallen victim to peer pressure simply because they wanted to fit in? What is missing? The answer to these questions is simple, it's a father. There are many differences between a child who grows up in single parent home and one who does not. In my opinion, the major difference is maturity. A child with an active father has a certain type of discipline that is instilled into the DNA of that child. The last thing a son wants to do is disappoint their Alpha Male so more than likely, they will think about the outcome when these types of situations arise.

A mother's love and discipline can only keep a child tamed for the moment, but an active father's wrath will last a lifetime. The night my friend knocked on my door, I knew it was a mistake, but these were my friends and they gave me what my father didn't. I felt obligated to give that same support back and that mindset has caused many athletes to never reach their full potential. That night could have changed everything and I would have been responsible for another fatherless child.

After I watched my friend empty his clip at a group of people on the corner that night, I nervously sat in class waiting for the day that I was questioned by the cops, or worse, retaliation. The beef between our crews continued and it wasn't safe. The level of hate increased and death was calling, I could feel it. I knew the devil was trying his best to keep me from God's promise, but I was still covered. A few weeks after the incident, hard knocks once again riddled my door.

"Yo, you coming?"

I dropped my head and mumbled, "Nah, I got too much to lose."

"Yeah you right, you don't need to be involved with this."

In shock, I closed the door. Even though I was worried about my friends, a huge weight was lifted off my shoulders. I didn't want my friends to be disappointed in me, but they cared for my future as much as I did and all I had to do was take a stand. Why is it so hard for our youth to take a stand? What are we as parents doing wrong? Are we too busy trying to keep up with Joneses ourselves that we give our children too much responsibility too soon? Lives are cut short, goals are never reached and futures never see the light of day all because we won't take a stand. I'm not perfect and it didn't come easy, but when I exercised my right to be an individual, I was finally freed from peer pressure.

After a few arrests and expulsions, the beef between our crews spilled over into one of my football games. It was a Friday night, the weather was perfect, and the bleachers were packed. Our rivals, Randallstown High School, were across the field and I wanted nothing more than to embarrass them. As if the rivalry wasn't enough, the running back for Randallstown High School was also involved in the altercation with my friends. I always tried to play with integrity, but on that night, I lost it and I tried to take his head off every chance I got. I wasn't going to settle our differences by shooting up his neighborhood, but the football field was a different story. It was a home game and even though I chose not to ride with my friends, they all expected me to put this boy in a coma. I didn't get a chance to lay him out, but I played a great game and the revenge was just as sweet.

129

My team was clearly going to win this game, so my coach pulled me out in the third quarter and I enjoyed watching their team deal with this embarrassing defeat. From the sideline, I heckled him like nothing I had ever done before and then it happened. They ran a sweep and my archenemy was running towards my sideline, but he was tackled. I jumped in his face and pushed him and that was the dumbest thing I ever did during a game. Coach Scriven snatched me up and tossed me like a feather.

"What the hell are you doing, Keion?"

I was so excited that I forgot that my actions would affect my team. We were penalized and I was suspended for the next game. My team was great, but I was the leader and without me, we weren't a threat to our opposing team. My anger cost us the chance to go to the playoffs, but more importantly, I left a terrible impression with the scouts. I was later told that I was perceived as an undisciplined, hot head from the streets of Baltimore and removed off their list.

After the game, I could barely eat from the guilt. I may have made my friends proud, but I disappointed my team and myself. Even though I loved the competitive nature of the sport and it helped me to deal with my anger, I promised myself that I would never play the game I love with uncontrollable hate again.

CHAPTER THIRTEEN

★★★

In my senior year, I had the world in my palm and a free education waiting for me – but there was one more obstacle I had to tackle, the Scholastic Aptitude Test also known as the SAT. I wasn't a dumb kid, but I heard stories of some of the brightest people performing miserably and settling for a mediocre education. I couldn't believe I had been in school all my life and my future depended on one test. Some of my friends who were gifted athletes were so intimidated by the SAT that they stopped pursing their dreams to play at the college level. I always loved a good challenge, but this was by far the hardest. In 1995, all a student needed was a score of 700 – which sounded like a piece of cake, but it wasn't.

The pressure I felt was unbearable and even though I had support from family and friends, the one voice I never heard was my father. I was destined to be the first student athlete to go to college in my family and my father missed it. He missed those talks at the dinner table; he missed every tackle, every interception, every pass, every catch, and every touchdown. He didn't pat me on the back when I messed up or kiss me on the forehead to soothe my thoughts. I needed him to tell me I was going to be okay. Is it fair to put all of my insecurities on my father? Yes, because I would have been a greater athlete, person, father, and man if he shaped me along the way.

Once again, I couldn't take my friends and family with me on this journey. It was me versus the SAT and I remember the day like it was yesterday. I walked into the crowded room and I sat down. This test was like nothing I had ever taken before. In high school, whenever a test was given, it took the teacher half the period to calm the class down, but not here. This was all business and it was extremely intimidating. The instructions were given, the time was set and all of our futures depended on it. As I stared at the clock, I nervously shook my pencil. My mind would often drift off as I watched other kids who seemed to zoom through their test. I criticized myself for all those nights that I chose to hang out instead of prepare for my future. Each student who finished their test before I did made me wonder if they grew up in a two-parent home. I closed my eyes, prayed and I hoped God would give me the answers, but even I knew that was a large order.

"You only have ten more minutes," the SAT coordinator shouted into the microphone.

I immediately began to panic and the sounds of my pencil tapping the wooden desk didn't help. The staff walked through the aisles like guard dogs and they were not there to help. If I had trouble

132

answering a question in class, all I had to do was raise my hand or tap the person next to me, but either one of those actions would disqualify me. I was on an island all by myself and that large clock on the wall was the countdown to my future.

"You only have one minute left," the SAT coordinator shouted.

"One minute?" I mumbled just loud enough to cause the student next to me to chuckle.

My future will be determined in one minute? I can hold my breath longer than that. I had three more pages to go, so I did the ole ABACADABA move and closed my SAT packet before the coordinator stepped up to the podium.

"Put down your pencils everyone and return your packet to the front."

I didn't want to move. All I could think about were all the answers I got wrong. It was over, and I felt like I failed. I was instantly outraged and instead of blaming myself, I blamed my dad.

"My father had become such a punching bag for displaced anger that I used him to deflect responsibility."

-K. Carpenter

I know there are some fathers out there who can relate to their son blaming them for everything. If this is happening to you, have you equipped your child emotionally to know better? At some point, your child will no longer have room for all the pain and disappointment and the missing parent will always get the blame.

Even though I made my decision on which college to attend, reality struck. *What if I didn't score well enough get in?* One Saturday morning, I pulled out the box that contained all the acceptance letters I received from different colleges. I sat Indian style on the floor and spread them around me. All these years, I envisioned myself playing football at a high level. I trained for it, received accolades and gained respect from my peers and coaches from all over, but none of it mattered. I didn't believe I performed well on the SAT and it was now time to start thinking about a Plan B. With an attitude and irritated beyond my wildest dreams, I opened up letters from Division II, III, and even Community colleges. I didn't want to disappoint my mother, so not attending a college wasn't an option.

Moments later, this feeling of defeat came over me and I could literally feel a cloud of sadness forming over my head. My plan since I was five years old was to prove to my father that I was worth knowing. My plan was to become so successful that he could no longer avoid me and I failed. How was my dad going to find me if I attended some Division III college in Delaware? How was I going to go to the National Football League if I attended a Community College? I am not talking down on those that have attended these types of colleges, but that wasn't for me. God gave me the athletic ability to be special and I felt like I let it all go to waste when I took the Scholastic Aptitude Test.

After thirty minutes of reading acceptance letters, my mother walked in. "What are you doing?" she asked.

I wanted to cry, but I never wanted my mother to worry because she dealt with so much. Unfortunately, I bared all the pain and disappointment I could take and I reached my breaking point.

My eyes filled up with tears. "I don't think I did well on my test."

"Yes, you did."

"I guessed the last few pages. I just drew a blank."

"Did you pray before you took the test?"

Afraid to look up, I just nodded my head.

"Then you gotta have faith."

My mother sat down next to me and placed her arm around my shoulder. I blamed my dad so much for not being there that I forgot my mother always knew how to give me the confidence I needed. Did I want this feeling to come from my father? Yes, but a mother's love is just as strong.

"I decided to go to Virginia Tech."

"So why are you looking through old mail?"

"Just in case I don't get in. I don't want to disappoint you."

"Keion, I don't care what school you go to. You are doing something that a lot of people do not get a chance to do and I am very proud of you. Now get up," she said with defiance. "God has a plan for you, do you believe that?"

135

"Yes."

She pulled me to my feet and one by one she picked up each acceptance letter, crumbled it, and basketball shot it into the trashcan. She missed the shot of course, but I loved her for always finding a way to make me smile. I crumbled up one of the acceptance letters and what started out as a "pitty party" turned into a basketball game with my mother. No matter how many people looked up to me, I was still that little breastfed baby to my mother. To this day, I still wonder how that moment would have turned out if my father would have walked into my room. What would he have said or was my mother all I needed?

To the mothers, never stop trying. You are not his father and sometimes, your attempts will fail simply because you are not his father, but never stop trying. I cannot emphasize that enough. Remember life is a collection of memories, so make sure you equip your fatherless child with plenty of great memories. When I was a depressed teenager staring at acceptance letters in my small bedroom, I didn't realize the lesson my mother was teaching me. I thought she was just being silly, but what my mother taught me was to have faith in God's plan. If I believed that it was in God's plan for me to play college football at Virginia Tech then claim it and give it to Him. I didn't know what she was teaching me until I reached my thirties. Life is a collection of memories and my mother knew I would recall this day and learn from it.

For weeks, I waited for the mailman to arrive. I sat on my front step and I was always a few minutes early. At 11:48 in the morning, I saw the mail truck in the distance and I immediately got butterflies in my stomach. I was a nervous wreck and each house he stopped at made me cringe. He was normally pretty fast, but for some reason that day he was moving extremely slow. He stopped to talk to neighbors and I badly

136

wanted to scream, "Hurry the hell up!" Finally, he reached my home and I didn't wait for him to get out.

"You've been meeting me outside for weeks. What are you waiting for?" he asked.

"My SAT scores. I gotta full scholarship, and you have my results."

"Well good luck, Keion."

"How do you know my name?"

The mailman laughed, "It's written on your mail, but I've also come to some of your games. You have a bright future." The mailman handed me the golden envelope.

This letter was the closet feeling to the Million Dollar Sweepstakes. I waited for weeks, but I was afraid to open it. My heart pounded and my mouth was dry. I walked into the house and my mother was sitting in the living room.

"You got it?"

"This is it," I replied.

"Well, open it!"

I ripped open the letter like an early Christmas gift and looked for my score. I scanned the piece of paper and my score was a 980. I dropped the letter, stepped back and my mother looked like she saw a ghost. There was a pause and silence then absolute mayhem. We embraced each other and jumped up and down like we won a championship. I couldn't believe it, little old Keion from Campfield was going to play college football for a primetime University. Everything I worked for, the summers I sweated in blistering heat and the nights that I threw the ball to myself all paid off. My mind was scrambled and I wanted to call everyone I knew. Within seconds of feeling the need to rejoice, reality struck once again like a bolt of lightning, *What about my friends? Who's going to watch my back and who's going to love me for me?* All I knew was about to change and a sense of fear came over me.

My mother was ecstatic and she called everyone. I picked up my SAT scores, walked into my room, and flopped onto my bed in disbelief. I did it. I made my family, my coaches and my friends proud, but that was just the beginning. In order for me to reach my goal in the National Football League, I had one more phase of my life to complete and I was more than ready. The pain and uncertainty I endured from being a fatherless child prepared me to face adversity head on. I wasn't perfect, I made my share of mistakes, but God's plan never wavered. When I was overwhelmed with doubt. He gave my mother the patience and the love to see me through. When I put myself in situations that could have put me in jail or in the grave, God's plan stood the test of time. I was covered when I thought I was alone. I was covered when I didn't believe in God's will. And I was covered when my father avoided his obligation. I am covered.

"Defy the odds."

—K.Carpenter

"Since I was a child, I was blessed through sports to look at my coaches as role models and father figures. If your son does not have a father figure, teach them to embrace their coaches."

—K. Carpenter

140

"Even as an adult, I learned to mask my pain through my smile."

—K. Carpenter

"Since I was a teenager, all I wanted to be was appreciated. I received many accolades, but nothing would have made me happier than a fatherly embrace after a great game."

—K. Carpenter

"I remember this day like it was yesterday. I played the biggest game of my life. I knew my college football days were coming to an end and the NFL was on the horizon. I thank God for every opportunity."

−K. Carpenter

"The brotherhood that I created in sports will last a lifetime. I could not imagine how my fatherless life would have turned out if I wasn't given the skills to fight through my confusion."

—K. Carpenter

"I remember leaving Baltimore and starting a new life in a new world. My skills on the football field secured my financial future, but there was still a hole in my heart."

—K. Carpenter

"When I entered the National Football League, I was dissappointed to see so many extrodinary athletes without their fathers. I asked myself, "When will it stop?"

−K. Carpenter

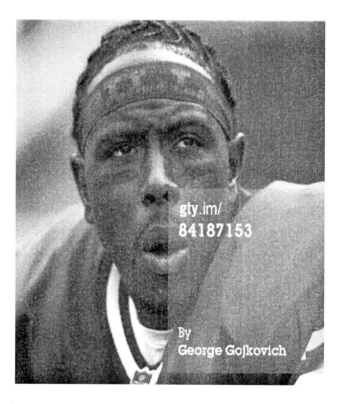

"The business of football is brutal. One minute you're buying a home and the next minute, you're on the plane to a new destination. Even though I had people in my corner, I would have loved to have a conversation with my father about my next move."

—K. Carpenter

"God has a plan for your child. What is in front of him or her is only momentary. When I was picked up by the Atlanta Falcons, I knew that was my final destination."

−K. Carpenter

"Parents, please love your child as their future depends on your love and support. He will make mistakes, but your love and discipline is truly the only remedy."

−K. Carpenter

"Trust your gut, fathers. Your presence will determine if your child reaches their full potential the easy way or the hard way."

—K. Carpenter

"To God be the Glory."

—K. Carpenter

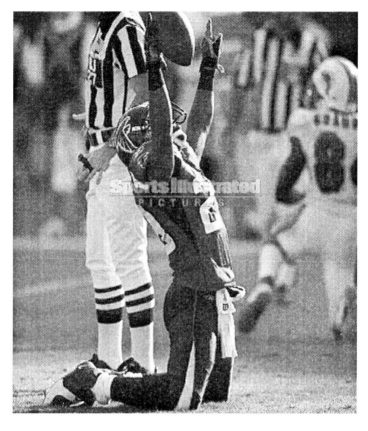

"I waited for this day, and whenever I got the chance to fall to my knees, I did."

—K. Carpenter

"It took me a while, but I learned that God's love was the perfect substitute for an absent father."

—K. Carpenter

"Even though my father didn't leave me with a legacy, I love him because he gave me the passion to start one. I love you pops. I vow to never allow my children to go through life without knowing I will always be there. I am no different. The love I have for my child, is no different than yours."

—K. Carpenter

I am convinced that my purpose in life is to shed light on this fatherless epidemic that has plagued our families for hundreds of years. I am more than willing to go where some fathers will not. I am dedicated to reminding all children, especially our sons, that it is okay and that it is not their fault. I am just like your son — I questioned my abilities, and I questioned if I was good enough. I hid my pain through my athletic abilities and even though it was the fuel to my fire, I would have given it all away to spend more time with my dad. The moment I held my first born in my hands, I knew I would never turn away. I would never plant the seed of doubt or the feeling of being unwanted.

I may not be there every step of the way, but my children will know daddy's love. To a child, our love is identical to the love and comfort that we feel from God. The same way that God died for us, we would die for our children and when that love is not evident, the outcome for that child can be detrimental.

Since I am an athlete, I decided to cater this book to a specific group of people. but I can only imagine how not having a father has affected those who do not have an outlet like sports. It is our responsibility to make sure that our fatherless children are not searching outside of their homes for love and acceptance. Cover your children the same way God has covered you. I hope you enjoyed reading this book as much I enjoyed sharing pieces of my life. Thank you again for taking the first step with me to end fatherlessness.